Teaching Jazz

A COURSE OF STUDY

MENC MUSIC EDUCATORS NATIONAL CONFERENCE

iaje
International Association of Jazz Educators

Developed by the International Association of Jazz Educators
Curriculum Committee

Gordon Vernick, Chair
Antonio García, Past Co-chair
Thom Horning, Past Co-chair

Curriculum Guide Editors:
Gordon Vernick, Geoffrey Haydon, Art Martin, Antonio García

Contributing Authors:
Jamey Aebersold, April Arabian-Tini, Russ Baird, Shelly Berg, Marcia Dunscomb, Richard Dunscomb, J. B. Dyas, Jeff Jarvis, Bart Marantz, Art Martin, Jesse McCarroll, Bernie Rose

Music Educators National Conference
1806 Robert Fulton Drive, Reston, VA 20191-4348

Printed in the United States of America
ISBN 1-56545-102-3

Contents

Acknowledgments

Only with the hard work of many could a project of this scope be completed. The International Association of Jazz Educators Curriculum Committee would like to recognize and thank the members of the following subcommittees for their contributions to this curriculum guide:

- Jazz in Instrumental Music: Art Martin,* John Arnn, David Baker, Sigi Bush, Patrick Crichton, Richard Dunscomb, Wayne Dyess, Remy Filipovitch, Antonio García, Becky Gillan, Mike Grace, Pat Harbison, Geoffrey Haydon, Bert Ligon, Bart Marantz, Ellis Marsalis, Daniel Murphy, Miles Osland, Chuck Owen, Jimmy Owens, Mike Parkinson, Ron Poorman, Frank Potenza, Peter Stigings, Ed Thigpen, Ken Tittelbaugh, Paula Zeitlin
- Jazz in Vocal Music: Antonio García,* Eva Adams, April Arabian-Tini, Russ Baird, Cathy Bleecker, Daniel Gregerman, Brian Lillos, Roger Treece, Michele Weir, Cheryl Brown-West
- Jazz in General Music: Jesse C. McCarroll,* Marcia Dunscomb, Stanley DeJarnett, Gene G. Suskalo
- Jazz Resource Development: Bernie Rose,* Art Davis, Richard Dunscomb, Marcia Dunscomb, Antonio García, Michael Parkinson, Ed Sarath, Chuck Tumlinson, Gordon Vernick, Michael West, Paula Zeitlin

* Denotes Subcommittee Chairperson

Foreword

Music educators today must be masters of teaching all aspects of music—from performance and improvisation to analysis and evaluation. Unfortunately, many music education graduates have no opportunity for training in jazz pedagogy. Others with a modicum of training are unsure of where to begin when developing a well-rounded music curriculum that includes a jazz improvisation component. Thanks to the emphasis on improvisation in the National Standards for Music Education, the value placed on this important creative skill is at an all time high.

I congratulate IAJE and MENC for the work they are doing to further the course of music education. As Artistic Director of Jazz at Lincoln Center, I look forward to working in partnership with these two important organizations on the development of a comprehensive course of study in jazz music for K–6 grade students, teachers, and preservice/music education students. With a goal of distributing the finished work to every elementary school in America, our objective is to acquaint teachers and their students with the full spectrum of jazz—its history, sociological importance to American culture, relationship to other curriculum areas, and its unique music vocabulary. It will complement the National Standards for Music Education and serve as an important resource to any K–6 music or general classroom teacher.

Teaching Jazz provides resources that can be immediately put into action in the music classroom. While their context is not intended to suggest a complete curriculum, these materials can be used to help in curriculum development, lesson planning, and assessment of music learning.

Published by the International Association of Jazz Educators (IAJE) and the Music Educators National Conference (MENC), *Teaching Jazz* is uniquely structured to cover six experience levels from the first-year teacher to the veteran jazz educator. Matched to each of these experience levels are eight key categories designed to meet the challenge of teaching what is historically an oral and aural tradition—ear training, rhythm, composition/improvisation, history, and theory, as well as keyboard, instrumental, and vocal skills.

Although each of these components will not necessarily receive equal instructional time, all are important ingredients in the recipe. Having said this, I strongly agree with the IAJE Curriculum Committee's assertion that *listening* to jazz is always the first and irreplaceable step in jazz education!

—Wynton Marsalis

Preface

In music education, there is a growing interest in establishing a jazz curriculum that will identify learning outcomes appropriate for the ages of the children being taught. As a result, music teachers are being asked to add jazz education to their curricula.

Teachers often contact the International Association of Jazz Educators (IAJE) or colleagues for assistance in developing courses in jazz education. In January 1989, a meeting in San Diego in conjunction with IAJE's International Conference explored developing courses in instrumental, vocal, and general music. From there, IAJE proceeded to generate a curriculum guide that could serve as a model for any school district. This guide would identify a sequence of outcomes for various ages and ability levels of music students.

Teachers with proven records of teaching success in jazz education were selected to participate in the vocal, instrumental, and general music task forces. As work progressed and the scope of the projects increased, a growing team of educators spent more than six years developing materials clear and concise enough to be helpful to teachers as they plan instruction. Additional professionals read rough drafts and responded to questionnaires.

The final document is not intended to be an "international" course of study; instead, it offers teachers a model for the development of sequenced learning outcomes that meet local needs. It also provides the novice teacher with guidance to start a jazz-oriented program in conjunction with any existing program. Organized in six levels, from Beginner (Level I) to Advanced (Level VI), it can be used at any age or grade level and is designed so students and teachers may work at their own pace.

IAJE does not suggest that this book be considered an all-encompassing document. What has been noted, however, by concerned IAJE officials for years is the need for a curricular guide about jazz education. When specific texts, discographies, or jazz literature are suggested in this document, they should not be considered as the only available sources. Also, these recommendations should not be considered as endorsements for specific authors, composers, compositions, recording artists, or texts.

IAJE hopes teachers find this document helpful in administering sequenced music instruction that results in easily measurable learning outcomes in jazz education.

How to Use This Curriculum Guide

Teaching Jazz is recommended for those educators (both first-year and experienced) seeking an overview of a comprehensive jazz program. At the same time, instructors seeking direction in offering even a single component or level of jazz education will find this guide a valuable resource and are encouraged to follow this model closely to ensure thorough coverage of the subject matter.

Many educators have requested IAJE support in outlining some reasons for jazz education. The opening chapter, "Rationales for Jazz Education," discusses many of the aesthetic and practical elements of jazz music and instruction. Other educators may wish to proceed directly to the chapter "Scope and Sequence of Instruction," a comprehensive grid summarizing a suggested approach to jazz instruction across the curriculum and through six levels of experience. A more detailed discussion of the ideas summarized in the grid is presented in the chapter "Teaching Recommendations" that follows it.

When interpreting the correlations offered by the summary grid, note that Level I is intended as an introductory level and is not correlated to a single school grade level. This takes into consideration the various school grade levels for band and vocal instruction. Likewise, one should not assume that all school programs will achieve a Level VI performance. The following grade clusters parallel those of other MENC curriculum guides:

IAJE Grade Cluster/Performance Level

School Grade Cluster	Performance Level
1–3	–
4–6	I–II
6–8/7–9	I–IV
9–12	I–VI
College/Post-HS	I–VI

The instruction of grades 1–3 and under is usually addressed within the related but differently focused scope of the general music curriculum. For this reason, a distinct "Jazz in General Music" chapter offers insights into the jazz education of the very young and inexperienced. Specific techniques and concepts targeting "Jazz in Instrumental Music" and "Jazz in Vocal Music" are explored in additional chapters of this book. *Teaching Jazz* concludes with "Resources for Jazz Education," a chapter filled with lists of books, journals, recordings, and other useful information.

Rationales for Jazz Education

- Jazz can and should be taught as aesthetic education.
- Jazz is a valid art form worthy of study and performance at all grade levels.
- Music education students need an understanding of the art form to teach jazz—it should be included in teacher preparation.
- Music education students should be encouraged to take a broadly based jazz pedagogy course.
- Aesthetics texts such as those by Meyer, Langer, and Reimer should be examined with the intention of applying aesthetic concepts to jazz and jazz-related music.

Jazz education can create a greater awareness of the value of jazz music and its influence on world culture. A person's individual musical taste is established by the high school years. Making jazz part of the general music curriculum promotes exposure and discourages prejudice against this art form. At the college level, a course requirement in jazz pedagogy for music education majors is recommended.

A central issue for jazz education is addressing jazz music as part of aesthetic education and its perceived role in music education. Many jazz educators think jazz education has not fulfilled its potential in music education. This may be due to the absence of a persuasive position on the "nature and value of jazz and jazz-related music" and, in turn, jazz education (Elliott, p. 164).

Jazz education must articulate a clear and precise philosophy based on aesthetic values of jazz. The aim of jazz education should be to develop in students a sensitivity to the expressive qualities of jazz as well as to provide opportunities for musical growth through creating, performing, and perceiving jazz. To this end, jazz education must be consciously aware of the depth of human understanding available to students through jazz education as aesthetic education. "Jazz education will become aesthetic education through an understanding of those elements that contribute to the unique musical qualities of jazz" (Brown, p. 34).

Some current concepts of music education as aesthetic education seem to be incomplete when addressing jazz and therefore are incapable of accommodating jazz and jazz-related styles. Some views of the value and importance of jazz as worthy of study seem to be outdated. This area needs attention to establish guidelines for teaching and learning jazz.

A review of philosophies offered in defense of jazz study reveals positions based loosely or not at all on the characteristics of jazz, though they may have practical value. Among them are the following:

1. Jazz is highly relevant to musical dialect of the twentieth century.
2. It is an American musical art form.
3. It requires specific skills, some used infrequently by other genres.
4. Jazz in the curriculum will upgrade musical standards.
5. It is an integral part of music education and American culture.

6. Improvisation will develop originality and creativity.
7. Jazz vocations are prominent in today's society.
8. Students develop a keen sense of pitch, rhythm, and other musical elements when studying jazz.
9. Jazz students are often better music theory students.
10. Jazz develops freedom with responsibility and leadership.
11. The contemporary music style aids student recruiting.
12. The economic overhead is generally far less than that of larger, nonjazz ensembles.

Jazz education can be aesthetic in nature if the following goals are considered and followed:

1. "To make jazz education aesthetic education, we must allow students to become sensitive to and discriminate among those musical elements that contribute to the aesthetic quality of jazz." Improvisation, timbre, rhythm, pitch, and other musical elements should become the focus of jazz education, along with an understanding of the historical and cultural concepts on which jazz is based.
2. "Jazz education as aesthetic education must be taught on its own terms, emphasizing those expressive qualities unique to the genre. To use a value system inappropriate to jazz is to ignore the intrinsic qualities of jazz" and to promote a biased and closed-minded approach to educational goals.
3. "The jazz curriculum must reflect the aesthetic aims of education. Creating, performing, analyzing, and perceiving jazz should be central to all jazz education programs, not as individual ends, but as part of a comprehensive curriculum aimed at developing an awareness of and sensitivity to the expressive qualities of the music" (Brown, p. 38).

Dual System of Aesthetics

The "essence of jazz lies in the simultaneous operation and appreciation of two aesthetic systems: African and Western European" (Elliott, p. 190). Jazz education must address these simultaneously. The philosophy of music education as aesthetic education seems to miss the essence of jazz and jazz-related music. It deals "effectively with Western European aspects" of jazz music but not "with the African musical dimension" that is the foundation of the jazz style (Elliott, p.188). The essence of the African musical aesthetic can be summarized as "without participation, there is no meaning" (Elliott, p. 232). The success of an African musical performance is inseparable from the degree to which the musicians and their music involve the audience and dancers, establishing a reciprocal musical relationship—each inspiring the other. "In jazz, the essence of this reciprocal relationship reveals itself in the way the musicians often inspire and respond to each other" (Elliott, p. 232) in their improvisations—and in the way an audience responds with verbal and physical acknowledgments (Elliott, 1985). "The relationship between social dancing and jazz in its infancy serves to obscure the real place of physical involvement in the history of this style."

"The nature and value of jazz is to be found in the characteristic ways the musical elements (melody, harmony, rhythm, tone color, texture, and form) are manipulated and emphasized to produce the jazz style" (Elliott, p. 184). Perception of and reaction to these musical elements and their combinations and interactions in individual examples constitute the basis for experiencing the embodied meaning of jazz selections. A keen awareness of these musical conditions "provides the basis for an aesthetic experience of jazz" (Elliott, p. 187).

"To deny a place in music education to jazz and jazz-related music" (Elliott, p. 262) would be to deny people access to forms that have the ability to develop human feelings in unique ways and to provide sources of significant and powerful music experience, insight, and import (Elliott, 1985). Jazz and jazz-related music—like all music—provide a focus for the myriad emotions, ideas, sensations, and impulses that constitute our being, such that through the music they are "re-fashioned and amplified into something new" (Elliott, 1985, p. 264).

In Eurocentric music, the composer and the performer each have a distinct function. In jazz there is no re-creator of the music. The improviser-performer as composer in jazz may be a stumbling block for the classically trained musician. "Like most other musical elements, pitch and timbre function in a unique way in jazz" (Brown, 1981, p. 37). Jazz musicians do not necessarily try to conform to a "conservatory" ideal sound. Their sound is unique and easy to identify. The unconventional sounds and characteristic tone quality produced by jazz musicians are an important part of the jazz aesthetic.

The fact that the emphases in jazz and jazz-related music are on improvisatory thinking and feeling, more than in most Western European art music, offers the possibility of transforming musical perception in unique ways. "Jazz education should be concerned with refining students' ability to perceive and react to the aesthetics of jazz" (Elliott, p. 266). The aesthetic experience of jazz and its most effective production depends upon immersion in the African dimension of musical performance. Jazz ought to be evaluated primarily in terms of the quality of its processual (rhythmic interaction) constructs.

Elliot sums up these characteristics in this way: "African-American music stresses processual meaning which is generated by the cumulative effect of rhythmic drive, spontaneity of performers' improvisations, and the placement of tones, accents, and gestures along a horizontal plane" (p. 193).

Some Conclusions

- There is a "significant lack of substantive foundations for the existence and practice of jazz education in the literature of music education and jazz education" (Elliott, p. 294).

- The musical meaning of jazz needs to be more clearly addressed in a philosophy of music education as aesthetic education (Elliott, 1985).

- Musical meaning in jazz is found in the "simultaneous operation and appreciation of two aesthetic systems: African and Western European—with an emphasis on the African components" that are "different in character and effect from the European" (Elliott, p. 295).

- "Jazz education as aesthetic education must develop a commitment to increase students' understanding of and sensitivity to the subtleties of the processual dimension of music" (Elliott, p. 300).

References

Bowman, Wayne. "Polayni and Instructional Method in Music." In *Journal of Aesthetic Education, 16*, p. 79. Summer, 1982.

Brown, T. Dennis. "Jazz Education as Aesthetic Education." In *Proceedings of NAJE Research Papers, 1*, 33–38. 1981.

Elliott, David James. *Descriptive, Philosophical and Practical Bases for Jazz Education: A Canadian Perspective.* Unpublished dissertation. Case Western Reserve University: 1985.

Franklin, Larry. *The Rationale for and Development of Jazz Courses for the College Music Curriculum.* Unpublished dissertation. Penn State University: 1981.

Hepworth, L.T. *The Development of a Course of Study in Stage Band Technique at the University of Utah for Inclusion in the Preparation of Secondary Instrumental Music Teachers.* Unpublished dissertation. University of Utah: 1974.

Newman, Robert. "Jazz Pedagogy for Music Majors." In *NAJE Jazz Research Papers, 2,* 107–112. 1982.

Reimer, Bennett. A *Philosophy of Music Education.* Englewood Cliffs, NJ: Prentice Hall Publishers, 1989.

Tracy, Michael. "Aesthetic Education and the Jazz Ensemble." In *NAJE Jazz Research Papers, 9,* 255–264. 1989.

Scope and Sequence of Instruction

Teaching jazz and ensemble performance is most effective when explored through the art form's many aspects. The comprehensive chart on the following pages is meant to be read as a whole. It classifies the jazz curriculum into eight categories that attempt to meet the challenge of teaching what is historically an oral and aural tradition:

- Ear Training
- Jazz Theory
- Rhythm
- Jazz Keyboard
- Composition/Improvisation
- Instrumental Skills
- Jazz History
- Vocal Skills

Each horizontal level (I–VI) represents a sequencing of material. Grade levels associated by MENC publications with this sequential division represent one possible application to age groups. However, this chart is not intended to be strictly related to age, as the variables of scheduling, class size, and abilities and experiences of students are critical factors. Whatever the organization of classes might be, these levels should be helpful as a guide for sequencing of instruction.

Ideally, most classes will proceed through the columns of the chart in parallel fashion. For example, the students would be learning first-level ear-training skills concurrently with first-level jazz-keyboard skills, and so on. It may be, however, that the instructor has only the most limited opportunity to meet with students. This chart outlines what initial exposure and activity might best be employed even for a single class meeting. Teachers may also wish to alter the sequencing based on the needs and abilities of any given group of students.

The chart format serves as a reminder that all components should be included in a quality jazz program. Although each component will not necessarily receive equal time during instruction, each must be present. Otherwise, for example, students might develop strong skills in jazz theory yet be unable to compose a melodic line or draw upon the creative work of their historic predecessors. As lesson plans are made and concerts planned, the teacher should incorporate all components of jazz education, keeping in mind that listening to jazz is the first and irreplaceable step in jazz education.

Level	Ear Training	Rhythm
I	Match pitches. Imitate simple rhythms. Imitate simple melodic patterns (especially call and response, blues riffs) with and without blues and Dorian accompaniment, incorporating Dorian and blues scale ideas.	Tap/clap unison beats and duple subdivisions. Tap/clap unison beats and triple subdivisions. Improvise individual tap/clap solos over unison beats. Listen to recorded examples of strong subdivisions within beats. Relate subdivisions to two- and three-syllable words.
II	Continue as above, increasing difficulty. Imitate melodic patterns with the "response" imitated also a half-step higher or lower than the "call." Identify/sing major, Dorian, and blues scales. Identify/sing major/minor chord tones. Play/sing pre-existing tunes by ear.	Tap/clap cross-rhythms of duple vs. triple subdivisions by dividing class roles. Improvise tap/clap solos over cross-rhythm beats. Improvise simple vocal/instrumental solos over cross-rhythm beats. Listen to recorded examples of cross-rhythm beats, including African tribal and contemporary. Explore swing, bossa, and samba grooves.
III	Identify/sing Aeolian and Mixolydian modes. Identify/sing dominant chord tones. Imitate simple recorded solos (modal or blues forms) vocally/instrumentally without written music. Introduce suggested scat syllables as needed. Continue imitation of more complex rhythms and melodies.	Tap/clap 6/8 clave beats using eighth-note cross-rhythms. Listen to and explore folkloric cross-rhythm beats such as Afro-Cuban "abakwa." Relate 4/4 swing pattern to 6/8 Afro-Cuban. Improvise simple vocal/instrumental solos over these beats. Explore recorded examples of swing, bossa, samba, shuffle, ballad, waltz grooves.
IV	Identify/sing pentatonic scales, remaining modes. Explore/imitate repetitive cross-rhythms over simple meter. Imitate simple recorded solos (AABA form). Imitate bass lines for simple vamps and progressions. Identify/sing intervals unison through fifth. Play/sing tunes from jazz repertoire by ear.	Tap/clap 3-2 clave beat, add cross-rhythms. Tap/clap 2-3 clave beat, add cross-rhythms. Listen to recorded examples of these beats in Latino music and Latino jazz. Improvise simple vocal/instrumental solos over clave beats. Explore recorded examples of above grooves. Transcribe from solos only simple rhythms and articulations.
V	Play/sing guide tones and bass tones to ii–Vs, iii–VI–ii–Vs, and dominant chord cycles. Continue imitation of melodic patterns, also re-creating them a half-step up or down. Continue to play/sing jazz tunes by ear.	Tap/clap cross-rhythms of 5/8 or 7/8 over 4/4. Listen to recorded examples of 5:4 and 7:4 in jazz. Improvise simple vocal/instrumental solos incorporating 5 or 7 over 4/4. Relate to 5- or 7-syllable phrases of words.
VI	Continue exploration of previous concepts. Play/sing guide tones and bass tones within tunes. Identify/sing/play whole-tone, diminished scales. Continue to play/sing jazz tunes by ear.	Explore bass-line constructions idiomatic to specific rhythmic patterns. Explore shifting easily from one cross-rhythm or subdivision to another. Improvise simple vocal/instrumental solos over shifting cross-rhythms or subdivisions.

Level	Composition/Improvisation	Jazz History
I	Recognize and use the concept of a theme, using 2- or 3-note ideas (with or without accompaniment). Recognize and use the concept of variation via dynamics, rhythm, articulation, timbre, etc. Invent simple themes. Explore "freestyle" improvisation (with or without accompaniment). Identify/learn tunes from jazz repertoire.	Hear and discuss recorded solos by Miles Davis ("So What"), Sonny Rollins ("Sonny Moon for Two"), and others who unify themes. Explore call-and-response style blues records. Hear scatting by Louis Armstrong, Ella Fitzgerald, and others. Listen to a variety of styles such as blues, Dixieland, swing, modal, funk, Latin, and bebop.
II	Explore tension and release by raising or lowering 2- or 3-note ideas a half-step (over unshifting modal or blues background), then returning. Explore "freestyle" improvisation over accompaniment, using major, Dorian, and blues scales. Identify/learn tunes from jazz repertoire. Analyze existing solos for creative content.	Hear and discuss recorded solos by Miles Davis, Thelonius Monk, and others who successfully exploit dissonant variations of themes. Explore recordings by Joe Williams, Sarah Vaughan, and others. Compare solos by different artists over the same tune. Listen to a variety of styles.
III	Improvise solos vocally/instrumentally over progressions similar to recorded solos imitated. Explore pacing of a solo. Compare written solos over simple progressions, then perform them. Identify/learn tunes from jazz repertoire. Analyze existing solos for creative content.	Continue blues/modal recordings. Explore AABA-tune recordings; discuss pacing of solos. Compare different versions of same tunes for creative choices. Explore recordings by Cleo Laine, Billie Holiday, and others. Listen to a variety of styles.
IV	Compose written bass lines for simple progressions, then perform them. Improvise bass lines. Explore cross-rhythms, thematic unity, and freedom of dissonance in improvised solos. Identify/learn tunes from jazz repertoire. Analyze existing solos for creative content.	Hear recorded bass lines. Explore African drumming recordings. Identify cross-rhythms within recorded solos. Explore more AABA-tune recordings, including rhythm changes. Explore recordings by Betty Carter, Jon Hendricks, Mel Tormé, and others.
V	Improvise over chord-cycle vamps and simple AABA tunes, including rhythm changes. Continue exploration of previous concepts. Compose written solos, then perform them. Identify/learn tunes from jazz repertoire. Analyze existing solos for creative content.	Hear a variety of rhythm-change recordings. Explore swing and bebop recordings using ii–Vs and iii–VI–ii–Vs. Continue exploration of vocal soloists and ensembles. Continue comparing solos by different artists over the same tune.
VI	Continue exploration of previous concepts. Explore "free" improvisation via imitation of peers over flexible accompaniment. Identify/learn tunes from jazz repertoire. Analyze existing solos for creative content.	Continue exploration of previous concepts. Hear recordings of "free," imitative qualities of performers such as Ornette Coleman and Ed Blackwell. Explore recordings by Ursula Dudziak, Bobby McFerrin, and others.

Level	Jazz Theory	Jazz Keyboard
I	Identify half and whole steps, simple meter, simple rhythmic notation. Explore melodic phrase concepts (antecedent, consequent, etc.). Identify numerical basis for basic I–IV–V blues progression.	Play simple melodic passages of half and whole steps by ear in imitation. Voice on keyboard root and seventh of basic twelve-bar blues progression.
II	Place notes on staff; identify thirds. Draw clefs. Identify 3/4 meter. Recognize simple key signatures. Identify major, Dorian, and blues scales. Explore further rhythmic notation. Identify chord symbol notation for major and minor chords.	Play major, Dorian, and blues scales. Play simple melodic passages. Voice major and minor chords. Voice simple progressions from the above, using root, third, and seventh.
III	Recognize additional key signatures. Identify Aeolian and Mixolydian scales. Identify chord symbol notation for dominant chords. Explore AABA, 32-bar form. Analyze simple solos for scale content. Transpose chord symbols to different keys.	Continue scales, melodic passages, and chord voicings in additional keys. Play Aeolian and Mixolydian scales. Voice dominant chords more fully. Voice simple progressions using all chord types thus far. Read basic tunes from lead sheets. Explore chord inversions.
IV	Recognize key signatures up to 4 sharps and 4 flats. Identify previous scales and modes up to 4 sharps and 4 flats. Identify remaining modes and pentatonic scale. Be able to identify intervals from unison through a perfect fifth. Define elements contributing to a strong bass line. Notate cross-rhythms and discuss where they "land."	Continue scales, passages, and voicings up to 4 sharps and 4 flats. Play pentatonic scales. Play written and improvised bass lines for blues and modal progressions. Voice given chord progressions. Play simple transcribed solos in the right hand while accompanying in the left hand. Transpose simple progressions to new keys.
V	Recognize additional key signatures and additional keys for scales and modes. Explore ii–V and iii–VI–ii–V cycle concepts. Apply cycle concepts to tunes from jazz repertoire. Analyze solos for cycle content.	Continue scales, passages, and voicings in additional keys. Voice ii–Vs and iii–VI–ii–Vs in several keys. Explore right-hand scales with left-hand chord voicings. Continue transposing simple progressions and basic tunes to other keys. Apply two-handed voicings.
VI	Recognize all key signatures. Identify previous scales and modes in all keys. Identify whole-tone and diminished scales in all keys. Identify additional chord symbols such as diminished and half-diminished. Apply chord/scale theory to tune analysis. Analyze solos for chord/scale content.	Complete performance of scales and voicings in all keys. Explore right-hand improvisation over left-hand chord progressions. Continue reading tunes of increasing difficulty. Continue tune transpositions.

Level	Instrumental Skills	Vocal Skills
I	Learn all basic individual instrumental skills within initial 12–18 months of instruction. Learn basic instrumental articulations within initial 6 months.	Sing simple jazz standards with good tone (using both aural and written examples). Explore gradually basic tone-production techniques (breathing, articulation, color, etc.). Sing in unison groups, gradually introducing concepts of ensemble blend and balance.
II	Explore vibrato technique and stylistic usage. Analyze differences between jazz and nonjazz articulation.	Sing basic vowels oo, ah, and consonants b, d, m, n, v. Explore basic solo, two-, and three-part singing. Sing roots of simple progressions and tunes via intervallic recognition. Build a repertoire of basic tunes. Emphasize motivic development in improvisation. Apply basic microphone techniques.
III	Imitate jazz phrasing and articulation found in recordings of various periods.	Examine voice for register breaks and smooth via exercises (including men's falsetto). Individualize warm-up routines. Sing roots and thirds of simple tunes and progressions. Explore vocal drum sounds, growls, and imitation. Examine proper style for repertoire. Explore resonance. Communicate verbally with rhythm section.
IV	Explore muted brass playing and vibrato vs. "dead" tone. Apply transposition to nonstandard keys. Continue imitating phrasing and articulation from advanced recordings.	Analyze basic physiology and develop behavior promoting vocal health. Begin or develop cultivated vibrato. Sing arpeggios of tunes and basic progressions (I–VI–ii–V). Play chord roots on piano while singing solo. Continue building repertoire, promoting blend, balance, and other aspects above. Sing in simple three- and four-part groups.
V	Continue transposition study. Analyze muted pitch problems in brass. Continue advanced phrasing imitations.	Apply selectively proper tone to given style. Develop facility singing bass lines. Modulate previous arpeggios through cycle of fifths, half-steps, etc. Develop greater understanding of rhythm section goals/needs; establish rapport. Continue building repertoire and all above aspects. Sing in four- to six-part groups.
VI	Continue to explore individual quirks of chosen instrument(s): specific notes causing pitch problems, alternate positions or fingerings, extended range, harmonic series, etc. Continue advanced phrasing imitations.	Accompany self on piano while singing. Sing in advanced four- to eight-part groups. Continue to develop all above aspects.

Teaching Recommendations

Topics in this chapter are based on information found in the chart in the preceding section. An in-depth discussion of each topic is beyond the scope of this book. Rather, this chapter offers a brief summary of points to keep in mind when implementing the items on the chart. (For more information, see other resources listed later in this guide.)

Ear Training

The ability to imitate ideas from others fosters the ability to recognize one's own ideas and realize them in voice or on an instrument. Ear training can begin by matching given pitches, imitating rhythms, and imitating simple melodies (especially in the call-and-response style rooted in the blues tradition). Ideas can be presented with or without chordal accompaniment.

Students should also develop the ability to alter a given idea by raising or lowering it a half-step. Introducing scales aurally for sing-back and playback can lead to their identification as a specific sound. As time passes, scales and rhythms offered should be increasingly more challenging.

The teacher can choose relatively simple jazz tunes for the students to learn by ear from a recording or live instrument or voice. (See the graded list of jazz tunes in the "Resources for Jazz Education" chapter.) As the students gain experience, additional tunes of increasing complexity should be learned aurally, and this should continue throughout the ear training sequence.

To develop recognition of the jazz-phrasing vocabulary, teachers should introduce students to the recorded solos of the masters and encourage them to sing along. Technically simple solos, such as Miles Davis's delivery of "So What" (*Kind of Blue,* Columbia CK40579), offer lyrical lines, daring rests, and a sense of overall pace—in addition to the ear training that comes from matching pitches and rhythms. These singing experiences also lower the inhibitions of students reluctant to experiment with improvisation.

Exploration of melodic intervals and imitation of root progressions can lead to singing and playing bass lines under static chords or simple progressions. As a longer-term goal, students eventually should be able to identify and construct guide-tone lines (connecting the thirds and sevenths of successive chords) and bass lines appropriate to a given tune. These tools will add experience and ability to any novice or intermediate improviser.

Rhythm

Rhythmic feel lies at the heart of any jazz—written or improvised. Students can begin by clapping a moderate pulse with other students and then adding duple or triple subdivisions. When an infectious beat takes hold, invite a student to improvise vocally or instrumentally over the "groove" (without any chordal accompaniment to hinder spontaneity). Encourage students to relate subdivisions to two- and three-syllable words that can form cohesive sentences and provide a basis for lyrical improvisation over this rhythmic tapestry. Expose the students to recorded examples of strong metric feels.

Cross-rhythms provide much of the tension and release associated with jazz phrasing. By dividing class roles, students can tap/clap duple subdivisions simultaneously with triple; and a student can tap/clap a rhythmic solo over this "groove." Soloists can add pitch by playing or singing. Again, exposure to recorded examples of cross-rhythms, from African tribal music to contemporary jazz, will bring the concept from passive thought to active life.

Creating the 6/8 meter from a 2/4 feel provides a link from Afro-Cuban rhythms and the Latino "clave" beat to what we term "swing." With the increasing interest in multicultural music, there are many recorded examples of these rhythmic feels available for your students. (A brief introduction might include the popular but authentic soundtrack from Tito Puente and others in *The Mambo Kings,* Elektra E2 61240; *Compact Jazz Dizzy Gillespie,* Mercury 832 574-2; and recordings by Chano Pozo, Mario Bauza, Paquito D'Rivera, and others.) Additional cross-rhythms of five or seven against four can be explored, relating to imaginative word phrases of the same number of syllables. And students can improvise rhythmic and melodic solos over any of these textures without benefit or restriction of chordal accompaniment.

When students have grasped a series of cross-rhythms and feels, challenge them to shift from one to another on your cue over a basic pulse. There are also traditional bass lines that are often constructed with certain rhythmic feels; students can benefit from coupling basic root movements to the beats. (See the Afro-Cuban and Latino examples listed above.)

Any exploration of rhythm has to include its application within a variety of historical jazz styles: swing, shuffle, bossa, samba, ballad, waltz, and others. Examine each for its primary and underlying pulses. Students can also transcribe *only* the rhythms and articulations of specific solos chosen for their application of model jazz styles.

By developing the ability to recognize, imitate, and vary superimposed rhythms, students learn to vary and superimpose their own rhythms on top of the "groove" provided by a rhythm section.

Composition/Improvisation

Good melodies are rooted in the principles of composition, and improvised melodies are spontaneous composition. Teachers wishing to develop strong improvisers must instill in their students a keen awareness and practical use of such concepts as theme, sequence, variation, tension and release, and pacing.

At the earliest stages of instruction, a teacher should expose students to the idea of theme, using only two- or three-note ideas (with or without accompaniment). Explore variation via changes in dynamics, rhythmic placement, articulation, timbre, and other possibilities. If a modal or blues accompaniment is employed (live or from a recording), lead students through tension and release by raising or lowering the simple theme a half step, then returning.

Improvisers will learn that a thematic idea is powerful enough to sustain dissonance—an important lesson whether the sound is intentional or created through a "mistake" while soloing. Encourage students to reuse any melodic "errors" immediately in their next phrase, repeating and then adjusting the "mistake" into consonance. This experience will greatly lower any inhibitions the students may have about improvisation.

Lead the students into "freestyle" improv, allowing them to play any related ideas using the scales eventually covered (starting perhaps with major, Dorian, and blues scales). All students should improvise vocally—scat singing—regardless of whether vocally or instrumentally rooted. The ability to identify one's own thoughts vocally, free from the habits and hindrances of a mechanical instrument, is a valuable tool toward freeing any improviser from existing limitations.

Students can compose written solos over simple chord progressions and perform them for critique. This allows them the opportunity to compare improvisation with compositional forethought and hindsight. Writing bass lines under progressions can lead to better spontaneous construction of them. This forces improvisers to focus on the crucial tones and scales of a passage or tune. As emphasized earlier, the imitation, transcription, and analysis of historic and contemporary solos by jazz masters will afford students perhaps their greatest insight into what makes fine solo construction: the creative unity of melodic ideas and chord/scale relationships. Improvisers of all ages must take every opportunity to "apprentice" from noted soloists in this way.

To study themes, go to the jazz repertoire itself. Choose from a wealth of Broadway and movie standard tunes, modal, blues, bossa nova, ballad, bop—even pop music brought in by the students. Despite an improviser's goal to create new melodies, too often we forget to examine the older, artfully crafted melodies right before our eyes. Not only do they provide style, they also lend a basis on which to build the first notes of improvisation. Most important, those students truly desiring to participate in a jazz career must memorize a vast number of tunes in order to keep up with demand. (See the graded tune list later in this document.)

As teachers expose students to increasingly challenging tune forms, ranging from modal vamps and blues to 32-bar tunes and "free" jazz forms, the improvisers will continually benefit from the opportunities of scat singing, constructing bass lines, writing solos, and, of course, improvising on their instrument of choice. Any experience students gain in the compositional process will benefit their improvisations.

Jazz History

Only with a perspective of one's predecessors and their accomplishments can an improviser mature as rapidly as possible. This is more than mere historical fancy, as the quest for "jazz phrasing" or a "jazz sound" leads directly to those persons who crafted this enviable vocabulary. So teachers must resist the urge to spend the limited class time strictly with textbooks, scales, or even creatively active exercises. Mentors must expose improvisers to the best examples of the art form. Otherwise, students are doomed to "paint the tree without having first seen one," a random exercise at best.

In keeping with the importance of compositional creativity, expose students to improvisers who consistently play solos of great thematic unity and clarity. Artists such as Miles Davis, Sonny Rollins, Louis Armstrong, and Ella Fitzgerald offer a wealth of recorded material demonstrating the influence of the blues on all forms of jazz. Artists such as Joe Williams, Sarah Vaughan, and Thelonious Monk offer a breadth of variation within their solo art. The style of works should evolve as the time line progresses to newer artists (who can also be inserted continually for comparison), and a variety of jazz grooves and styles should be incorporated into the journey. (A list of suggested recordings can be found in the chapter "Resources for Jazz Education.")

By comparing different recorded versions of the same tunes, students can realize and begin to understand the creative choices made even when presented with the same raw material. The variation in the delivery of the tune itself, added to comparisons of the artists' solos, provides clear opportunities to discuss how historical artists viewed their creative processes.

African-drumming recordings display cross-rhythms relevant to the current jazz language. Vocal artists such as Betty Carter, Jon Hendricks, and Mel Tormé offer instant examples of rhythmic invention in improvisation, as do vocal and instrumental ensembles. The swinging traditions of the Duke Ellington and Count Basie orchestras provide a solid perspective on two of the most influential ensemble leaders in jazz.

The language of bebop, ii–V–I progressions, is aptly demonstrated by historical artists such as Charlie Parker and Bill Evans. "Free" jazz, championed by Ornette Coleman, Ed Blackwell, and Don Cherry, is still rooted in the communication of theme and mood.

Any exposure to jazz history you provide your students will affect their active jazz vocabulary. Without such exposure, improvisers are limited to the stimuli they themselves can create.

Jazz Theory

The creative right brain provides spontaneity and direction, but the methodical left brain provides the focus and accuracy essential to constructing a balanced solo. Just as ignoring the elements of creativity can produce sterile, mechanical-sounding solos, ignoring theoretical principles can lead to unresolved ideas that might otherwise have been effective.

Introduce elements of traditional theory first: half and whole steps, simple meter, simple rhythmic notation, and melodic concepts such as antecedent-consequent (or call and response). The numerical I–IV–V basis for the basic blues progression can lead to listening for those chord shifts. After introducing the staff, discuss details of pitch placement, clefs, meter, and key signatures and then introduce basic scales such as major, Dorian, and blues.

The chord symbols used in jazz will demand special attention, both for their construction of stacked-thirds and their corresponding scales. As teachers expand the range of key centers, new scales and modes come into play; students should learn to transpose chord symbols to different keys. Exploration of cross-rhythms and where they again "land" on the downbeat of a bar relates directly to their uses in improvisation.

As knowledge about chords and scales improves, teachers can choose tunes for students to analyze for chord and scale applications. A wider scope of intervals and scale study (including pentatonics) can lead to study of the ii–V–I and iii–VI–i–V–I progressions. The "Tin Pan Alley" jazz repertoire is filled with songs built on these cycles; the students can also examine such tunes for these progressions. Whole-tone, diminished, and half-diminished scales not regularly exploited in traditional theory prove important in jazz. Students can analyze recorded solos of major artists for the appearance of these and other sounds. And there is no end to the harmonic-substitution principles that can be applied and interpolated in the jazz vocabulary.

By exposing students to the forces inherent in jazz theory, teachers give improvisers the opportunity to understand cause and effect in the sounds they hear.

Jazz Keyboard

While the language of jazz is open to all instrumentalists and vocalists, concepts of melody and harmony are more visible on a piano or keyboard instrument. Students can also learn practical accompanying skills in piano study—skills that benefit composition and arranging. And though today's synthesizers and sequencers can be driven from many instruments, keyboards provide a ready access for even the novice musician.

Students can begin by playing simple melodic passages of half and whole steps by ear in imitation of the teacher's example. By using a limited note-pool, numerous variations are possible to develop the students' abilities to identify pitch relationships and lower their inhibitions. At the youngest ages, students can begin these exercises using mallet and Orff instruments, welcome "toys" for this compositional "game." Root and seventh voicings for basic blues progressions can be taught or guided visually by voicing chords on the piano as the students follow.

Learning simple scales on the piano provides a strong visual perspective. Major, Dorian, and blues scales are an excellent place to start. Simple theme imitations can then be drawn from those scales as a learning tool. By adding simple voicings of major and minor chords in the left hand, a student experiences the relationship of melody and harmony. Voice simple progressions drawn from these chords.

As time passes, students should learn those scales and chords in more key centers and add more of the modes drawn from those scales. Additional chord/scale relationships, such as the dominant chord and Mixolydian scale, should soon follow. Students can also apply the principles of bass-line construction (as discussed earlier) at the keyboard under one-chord vamps or simple progressions. They can play chord voicings in the left hand while reading simple, transcribed solos in the right hand. And they can transpose basic progressions to different keys.

The ability to voice ii–V–I and iii–vi–ii–V–I progressions at the piano is crucial to internalizing their musical influence quickly. With limited key centers, application of right-hand scales over the left-hand progression can be explored. Eventually, students should be able to accomplish this in all keys. By continuing tune transpositions and also applying two-handed voicings, students grasp skills that will be useful in accompanying themselves or others.

Throughout the process, teachers can show students simple tunes to play with both hands at the piano. Combining the experiences of voicing chords and learning scales with the improvisational experiences discussed earlier in this chapter, students can explore simple right-hand improvisation over left-hand chords from the tune at hand. Developing the ability to visualize the merging of melody and harmony will assist the soloing skills of any "single-line" instrumentalist or vocalist—as well as cultivate the ability to accompany and transpose tunes as needed.

Specific Instrumental and Vocal Skills

For additional information regarding applications of techniques specific to instrumental or vocal jazz education, see the "Jazz in Instrumental Music" and "Jazz in Vocal Music" chapters of this guide.

Jazz in General Music

Why teach jazz to young children? We can teach jazz and improvisation successfully to children from preschool through elementary grades. Historically, we have presented the concepts of music in a pre-reading setting whereby students learn to experience and enjoy the music, identify specific musical elements, and create their own music on a variety of instruments. From the first successful experiences, the children begin to identify musical symbols as a preparation for reading.

Expressing oneself musically is as natural as expressing oneself verbally. With a little encouragement in the proper setting, this expression can be the beginning of a lifetime of musical enjoyment and satisfaction. Children learn to speak and express thoughts for several years before facing the challenges of reading and writing. As teachers, we can address the language of music in the same way. We frequently observe children expressing themselves when at play. We can build on this easily, but must take care to make it a positive and "fail-proof" experience. Students in lower grades can make up stories and describe them through sounds on their instruments or with hands and body movements. Remember students are creating their own music, so whatever they do is correct; they should not be told anything is "wrong." Avoid being critical of their efforts lest we teach students to fear making a mistake and they become reluctant to participate.

In the early grades, especially kindergarten, the teacher can use short selections. Children can use hand, arm, and body movements (such as skipping, jumping, and swaying) in some of their activities. These movements help them understand high and low (range) and soft and loud (dynamics) elements.

One of the best sources for rhythms in the early elementary grades is *Thresholds to Music Programs* by Mary Helen Richards (Fearon Publishers; Belmont, California, 1964). Although this is not a recent publication, it is still very popular. Jamey Aebersold's *Play-Along Series* can be used on many different levels. The teacher can block out instruments and use what is appropriate for a given situation. To help get students in the mood for experiencing rhythms, the teacher should play different recordings of Gershwin's "I Got Rhythm" and discuss them. Another excellent book for the very young is *Melody Maker* by Marcia Dunscomb. This offers many creative activities for students as well as piano accompaniments for each lesson. A classroom teacher with limited piano skills will be able to play these pieces. This pre-reading method book introduces students to many concepts that are clear and easy to comprehend without reading notes. See the Jazz Pedagogy Resources list in the final chapter for full details on Dunscomb's book.

Equipment Needed

While an acoustic piano is desirable, the availability of small, inexpensive keyboards has made the keyboard a natural classroom resource. Mallet instruments such as Orff instruments also work well. In addition, a collection of rhythm instruments (drums, claves, triangles, etc.) will give the instructor the ability to keep everyone actively involved. Older students should be introduced to the bongo, conga, timbales, and other rhythm instruments such as tin cans, bottles, graters from the kitchen, and spoons to create sounds heard in Brazilian music. Vocal activities will make the experience more complete and enjoyable. Including jazz and improvisation in the daily classroom activities can enhance all early education and become one of the favorite classroom activities for students and the teacher. A small collection of jazz CDs suggested here will provide the classroom instructor with a basic collection for listening. Recordings by Willie Colon, Mongo Santamaria, Dizzy Gillespie, Eddie Palmieri, Paquito D'Rivera, Frank Grillo (nicknamed Machito), and many others can be used to introduce styles such as salsa, bomba, plena, bossa nova, samba, merengue, rhumba, cumbia, Cubop, boogaloo, and Latin rock. Encourage students to play rhythms along with some of the recordings. Children like rhythmic and energetic music. The following list is only a suggestion; many other jazz CDs would work just as well. The CD format is recommended because it is easy to use. A portable CD player is adequate for classroom use.

CD List

April in Paris. Count Basie. Verve 825-575-2.

The Best of Herbie Hancock. Blue Note CDP7-91142-2.

Bird: The Original Recordings of Charlie Parker. Verve 837-176-2.

Giant Steps. John Coltrane. Atlantic 1311-2.

Groovin' High. Dizzy Gillespie. Savoy SV-0152.

Kind of Blue. Miles Davis. Columbia CK40579.

Major and Minor, Vol. 24. Jamey Aebersold. JA1238D and JA 1237D.

Night Train. The Oscar Peterson Trio. Verve 821-724-2.

Paris, 1958. Art Blakey and The Jazz Messengers. Blue Bird 61097-2.

Play. Bobby McFerrin and Chick Corea. Blue Note D105634.

Satin Doll. Duke Ellington. Eclipse 64020-2.

Saxophone Colossus. Sonny Rollins. Prestige OJCCD-291-2.

Stan Getz and Friends. Verve 835-317-2.

Time Out. Dave Brubeck. Columbia CK40585.

The following guideline suggests a structure for presenting the concepts of music in jazz. The text used for this suggested outline is Dunscomb's *Melody Maker.* Each activity can be repeated many times, varied, and expanded at each repetition. Children love to repeat familiar activities they enjoy. Systematic review ensures success. Evaluate the learning capability of your students and take them only as far as they can go successfully. Many concepts can be covered in one class, and the same concept can be covered in many different ways. Each class should be made up of about seventy-five percent review and twenty-five percent new material that builds on the previously learned skills. The pre-reading skills should not be confused with "rote" teaching.

CONCEPT	EAR TRAINING/ LISTENING ACTIVITY	KEYBOARD/MALLET INSTRUMENT ACTIVITY	RHYTHM INSTRUMENT ACTIVITY	VOCAL ACTIVITY	PREREADING/ READ ACTIVITY
Music has a steady beat.	Listen to a jazz tune such as "Driftin'" *(The Best of Herbie Hancock)*.			Say: "Beat, beat, beat, beat," ♩ ♩ ♩ ♩ on each steady beat as you listen. Clap on each beat.	Use a visual aid of a flash card with 4 bars of equal length to represent the steady beats: — — — — Some students can tap on the bars as the music plays.
Music has a steady beat	Listen to a jazz tune such as "Bag's Groove" *(Night Train)*.		Play a steady beat on claves or drums with recording.		
Music has a steady beat.		Play Aebersold (Vol. 24/Disc 1/Track 2). Have some students play a steady beat on "C."	Other students play a steady beat on rhythm instruments.	Other students chant "Beat, beat," etc.	
Music has a steady beat.	Listen to a jazz tune such as "Blues March" (Paris, 1958).				Use a visual aid of a flash card with 4 large quarter notes. Students tap the steady beat on the notes.
Music has a steady beat.		Play Aebersold (Vol. 24/Disc 1/Track 2). Have all students chant while one student makes a melody on the white keys to the rhythm pattern: "Mu-sic Has a Stead-y Beat, Yes." ♩ ♩ ♩ ♩ ♩ ♩ ♩ ♩	Other students play steady beats on rhythm instruments.	Other students chant "Mu-sic has a stead-y beat, yes." ♩ ♩ ♩ ♩ ♩ ♩ ♩ ♩	
Music can have rhythm patterns.		Play a melody on the black keys to the rhythm pattern: "Short, short, long-hold." ♩ ♩ 𝅗𝅥 (see *Melody Maker*, page 8).		Clap and say "Short, short, long-hold," ♩ ♩ 𝅗𝅥 while some students play this pattern on keyboard.	Use a visual aid of a flash card with bars representing the Short, short, long pattern. — — ——
Music can have rhythm patterns.	Listen to a jazz tune such as "Blue 7" *(Saxophone Colossus)*.		Some students play this rhythm pattern on rhythm instruments while others clap and chant.	Begin by clapping and Begin by clapping and chanting on every beat, "Beat, beat, beat, beat." ♩ ♩ ♩ ♩ Then change to: "Short, short, long-hold." ♩ ♩ 𝅗𝅥	Use a visual aid such as a flash card with "Quarter, Quarter, Half Note." Have students tap rhythm pattern on notes.

CONCEPT	EAR TRAINING/ LISTENING ACTIVITY	KEYBOARD/MALLET INSTRUMENT ACTIVITY	RHYTHM INSTRUMENT ACTIVITY	VOCAL ACTIVITY	PREREADING/ READ ACTIVITY
Music can have rhythm patterns.	Listen to Aebersold (Vol. 24/Disc 2/Track5). Listen for places where "Short, short long-hold" can be heard in the piano "comping." The comping pattern changes but students can continue the "Short, short, long-hold" anyway.	Play Aebersold (Vol. 24/Disc1/Track 5). Have one student play a melody on the black keys while all students chant the rhythm pattern: "Short, short, long-hold." ♩ ♩ 𝅗𝅥 Place a sticker on A flat and tell the students this is the "home" key that they can return to.	Other students play the rhythm pattern on rhythm instruments.	Other students clap and chant "Short, short, long-hold." ♩ ♩ 𝅗𝅥	
Music can have rhythm patterns.	Listen to Aebersold (Vol. 24/Disc 2/Track 4). Clap and chant the rhythm pattern: "Mon-keys like to eat a banana."	Play Aebersold (Vol. 24/Disc 2/Track 4). Have one student play a melody on the black keys: "Monkey Blues" (see *Melody Maker*, page 10).		All students chant the rhythm pattern: "Mon-keys like to eat a ba-na-na." ♩ ♩ ♩ ♩ ♪ ♩ ♪ ♩ ♩ (The syncopation is no problem for the students if they have lyrics to help them.)	
Music can have rhythm patterns. Incorporate these activities into your lesson plans as the students are ready.	Either/or ear training: Tell students you are going to play one of the following four rhythm patterns, and have them identify the one they hear: "Short, short, long-hold" ♩ ♩ 𝅗𝅥 "Long-hold, short, short" 𝅗𝅥 ♩ ♩ "Short, long-hold, short" ♩ 𝅗𝅥 ♩ "Short, short, short, short." ♩ ♩ ♩ ♩ You can begin with only two rhythm patterns; as the students are successful hearing the two, add a 3rd and finally a 4th. Keep all experiences successful.		Have students make melodies using the rhythm patterns they choose.		Have students take rhythmic dictation by making "long" or "short" marks on the board. When students are ready, dictate two-measure phrases. Use flash card with bars representing the rhythm patterns. Have students write their own pattern of long and short bars. Everyone can clap and chant the rhythms. The rhythm patterns can be used for melodic improvisation.
Music can have rhythm patterns.		There is no limit to the rhythm patterns that can be utilized for melodic improvisation.			
Music can have rhythm patterns. Incorporate these activities into lesson plans as students are ready.		After students are comfortable recognizing note values and clapping and counting, let them write 4-beat patterns and use them to improvise their own melodies. Choose a track from Aebersold, Vol. 24, in C major or A minor for white-key improvisation. Choose a track in D-flat major, G-flat major, E-flat minor, or B-flat minor for black-key improvisation.			Prereading training: Introduce note value flash cards and have students count the number of beats. Begin with the whole note. Count 1,2,3,4 for each whole note. Next introduce the half note and count 1,2 for each half note. Next introduce the quarter note and count 1 for each quarter note.

CONCEPT	EAR TRAINING/ LISTENING ACTIVITY	KEYBOARD/MALLET INSTRUMENT ACTIVITY	RHYTHM INSTRUMENT ACTIVITY	VOCAL ACTIVITY	PREREADING/ READ ACTIVITY
Music can be in a high or low register.	Play high or low melodies on the keyboard, and have students reach high or low in response.	Let students choose whether to play their own melody in high or low register of the keyboard.		Have students sing a familiar melody as high as they can. Have students sing a familiar melody as low as they can.	Let students point to a treble clef sign when they hear high melodies and to a bass clef sign when they hear low melodies.
Music can be in a low register. **Music can have call & response.**	Listen to "So What" *(Kind of Blue)*. Have students chant "Well mu-sic can be very low" with the bass line. Have other students chant "Oh Yeah" with the response chords. 𝄾 ♪ ♫ ♫ ♫ 𝅝	Let one student improvise a low register melody to this rhythm pattern while some other students clap and chant the rhythm pattern "Well music can be very low" and other students clap and chant "Oh Yeah."		See keyboard activity.	
Music can be in a low register.	<u>Either/or ear training:</u> Play something, and ask students to tell you if they heard a low or high register. Play "Blue 7" *(Saxophone Colossus)* and have students listen to the low register of the opening bass solo.	Play Aebersold, Vol. 24/Disc 2/Track 5. Have one student improvise a low melody on the black keys to the rhythm pattern: "Mu-sic can be low-hold-hold-hold." ♩ ♩ ♩ ♩ 𝅝		Other students clap and chant: "Music can be low-hold-hold-hold." ♩ ♩ ♩ ♩ 𝅝	
Music can be in a high register.	Listen to a jazz tune such as "Blue 'n' Boogie." *(Groovin' High)*. Have students listen to the high register of the trumpet. Reinforce previously learned concepts such as steady beat.		Always keep students who are not the "soloist" involved by having them play a specific rhythm pattern or steady beats on a rhythm instrument. Be careful that the rhythm instruments don't drown out the soloist. The end result should be musical.	Always keep students who are not performing involved by having them clap and chant as their classmates take turns being the "soloist."	
The steady beat can be fast or slow.	Listen to jazz tunes such as "Groovin' High" *(Groovin' High)*, "Kim" *(Bird)*, "Lover Man" *(Bird)*, and "Flamenco Sketches" *(Kind of Blue)*. Clap the steady beat and identify as fast or slow.		Play steady beats on rhythm instruments. Change from fast to slow tunes and have students be able to follow beat.		
Music can be higher or lower in a narrow range.		Play Aebersold, Vol. 24/Disc 2/Track 11. Place stickers on two "D"s on the keyboard an octave apart and alternate playing the lower and higher ones as you say: "Low-hold-hold; High-hold-hold." 𝅗𝅥. 𝅗𝅥.			

CONCEPT	EAR TRAINING/ LISTENING ACTIVITY	KEYBOARD/MALLET INSTRUMENT ACTIVITY	RHYTHM INSTRUMENT ACTIVITY	VOCAL ACTIVITY	PREREADING/ READ ACTIVITY
Music can have melody patterns that step.	Listen to “Blue Rondo a la Turk” *(Time Out)* and listen to the stepping pattern in the theme. Listen to “Honey Dripper” *(Night Train)* and listen to the two-note stepping pattern in the bass. Listen to “Moritat” *(Saxophone Colossus)* and listen to the stepping pattern.	Play Aebersold, Vol. 24/Disc 2/ Track 11. Place stickers on two “D”s on the keyboard and play: “Low-step-step; High-step step.” ♩ ♩ ♩ ♩ ♩ ♩		Have students sing three-note patterns that step up or down. They can sing scale degrees: “1, 2, 3, 2, 1;” Solfège: “Do, re, me, re, do;” or Pattern: “Play, step, step, step, step.”	<u>Prereading training:</u> Introduce the staff and let students learn that note heads can be on lines or in spaces. A large staff drawn on paper with poker chips for note heads will work well. In future classes, position the chips in stepping patterns. This is nonspecific notation and students can try to play these patterns on white keys.
Music can have melody patterns that skip.	<u>Either/or ear training:</u> Ask students to listen to short patterns and tell you if they heard steps or skips.	Same as above but: “Low-skip-skip; High-skip-skip.” ♩ ♩ ♩ ♩ ♩ ♩		Have students sing three-note patterns that skip up or down. They can sing scale degrees, solfège, or pattern.	Same as above but position the chips in skipping patterns.
Music can have melody patterns that skip and step.		Same as above but let each student decide on a pattern of skips and steps to use for their melody.			Same as above but position the chips in patterns with skips and steps.
Music can be loud or quiet.	Play a jazz tune such as “Take Five” *(Time Out)* or “Billie's Bounce” *(Stan Getz & Friends)*. Teacher adjusts volume from loud to quiet and students stand when they hear loud, sit when they hear quiet.				Students can point to flash cards that say “forte” or “piano” to indicate when they hear loud or quiet.
Music can be loud or quiet.		Review “Monkey Blues.” Student plays loud or quiet as teacher adjusts the volume of accompaniment to follow the student's lead.	Other students playing rhythm instruments must listen to soloist and respond accordingly.		
Music can have melody patterns that go up.	Listen to “Moritat” *(Saxophone Colossus)* and listen to ascending pattern. Have students shape pattern in the air as they listen.	Review “Monkey Blues.” Student begins the phrase each time in a middle register and move upward.			
Music can have melody patterns that go down.	<u>Either/or ear training:</u> Play short examples of ascending or descending lines and have students tell you which they heard. Listen to “Blue Bossa” *(Play)*. Listen for descending pattern. Listen to “Giant Steps” *(Giant Steps)*. Raise your hand when you hear a descending pattern.	Review “Monkey Blues.” Student begins the phrase each time in a high register of the keyboard and moves downward.			

CONCEPT	EAR TRAINING/ LISTENING ACTIVITY	KEYBOARD/MALLET INSTRUMENT ACTIVITY	RHYTHM INSTRUMENT ACTIVITY	VOCAL ACTIVITY	PREREADING/ READ ACTIVITY
Music can have melody patterns that go up and down.	Listen to "Mr. P.C." *(Giant Steps)*. Listen for pattern that goes up and down.	Let students improvise melodies that go up and down.			Let students draw the shape that they plan to use in their improvisation.
Music can have melody patterns.	Listen to "Now's the Time" *(Bird)*. Listen for the soloist to play a pattern and then repeat it. Ask students to see how many repeated patterns they can hear.	Let students choose a melody pattern such as: "Play, step, step, skip." The teacher can have several patterns written on flash cards for students to select from for the first experience. Play Aebersold, Vol. 24/Disc 1/Track 2. Have students play their melody pattern on the white keys, beginning in a new place each time.			
Music can have repeated patterns.	Listen to "Woodchoppers Ball," "Stompin' at the Savoy," "In the Mood," or "Flying Home" *(Big Band's Greatest Hits)*. Point out the beginning melodic pattern. Have students listen for the repeat of this pattern.	Let students choose a melody pattern and build their improvisation around repeating this pattern.			
Music can have repeated notes.	Play "C Jam Blues" *(Night Train)* or "Con Alma" *(Stan Getz & Friends)*. Have students raise their hands when they hear the repeated note theme pattern.	Choose an Aebersold track for black-key improvisation (such as Vol. 24/Disc2/Track 1). Encourage students to use repeated notes in their improvisation.			<u>Prereading training:</u> With paper staffs, let students place chips in repeated note patterns.
Music can have melody patterns that are repeated.	Play "Cantaloupe Island" *(Herbie Hancock)* and listen for repeated pattern in bass as well as repeated melody patterns.	Let one student create a bass pattern on the white or black keys. Let another student improvise melodies over this "ostinato."		Have students say the "pattern" that was created. (i.e., "Play, skip up, step down, repeat").	<u>Prereading training:</u> Have students draw the shape of the bass pattern.
Music can have melody patterns that are inverted.		Let students create a melody pattern that ascends and then invert it. Choose an Aebersold track for white-key improvisation and let students improvise using patterns and inversions.		Say the pattern: "Play, step up, step up, skip up." Now say the inversion: "Play, step down, step down, skip down."	<u>Prereading training:</u> On paper staff, let students place their chips in a pattern and then invert it.
Music can have melody patterns and sequences.	Play "Now's the Time" (Paris, 1958) and listen to the sequences in the introduction. Play "Satin Doll" *(Satin Doll)* and listen to the sequence of the opening theme (after the introduction).	Let students create a melody pattern and improvise using sequences of their pattern.		Have students say their pattern as they create sequences.	<u>Prereading training:</u> On paper staff, let students place their chips in a pattern and then place more chips in a sequence.

CONCEPT	EAR TRAINING/ LISTENING ACTIVITY	KEYBOARD/MALLET INSTRUMENT ACTIVITY	RHYTHM INSTRUMENT ACTIVITY	VOCAL ACTIVITY	PREREADING/ READ ACTIVITY
Music can have melody patterns that are incomplete (fragments).		Let students create a melody pattern and then use fragments of it in repetitions and sequences for their improvisation.			<u>Prereading training:</u> On paper staff, let students place their chips in a pattern and then remove some chips to create a fragment.
Music can have melody patterns that are made longer (extensions).		Let students create a melody pattern and then use it like the first words in a sentence, adding a different ending each time.			<u>Prereading training:</u> On paper staff, have students place their chips in a pattern and then add more chips to it to create an extension.
		Keyboard Geography: ABC Blues. Have one student play the bass pattern "A, G, F, E" while another student improvises a melody on "A, B & C."			<u>Prereading training:</u> Use a paper staff with a bass clef on it. Place a chip on the first space "A." Now place chips on "B" and "C."
Music can have chord progressions.		Let one student play the root tones for a simple chord progression such as C, F, G, C. Have them hold each note for 4 beats in the low register while another student improvises on the root note and its neighbors. This can evolve to 12-bar blues progressions and other chord progressions.			
Music can be in a major or minor tonality.	<u>Either/or ear training:</u> Play a major pattern followed by the major pattern again or a minor pattern. Ask students to identify "same" or "different." <u>Either/or ear training:</u> Play a major or a minor pattern for students to identify.	Play the first three notes of the white-key major scales (C, F, G); identify this as a major sound. In subsequent classes, try to play the first three notes on A, D, and E and discover that black notes are needed to make a major sound. In subsequent lessons, improvise on all major patterns, all minor patterns, etc.		Sing "1, 2, 3" on the first three pitches of these major scales.	

All music concepts can be explored and internalized in an improvisational setting. Once the students are assured of their ability to make music, reading is the next logical step. Since we haven't taught anything that needs to be "untaught" or "relearned," it is an easy progression from the prereading activities to reading notation. There is no time limit for accomplishing these skills, and every class will develop at a different pace. The only rule is to keep it positive, successful, and fun. The worst thing we could do at this point would be to make children feel as if they shouldn't study music.

Additional Suggestions

Have students create phrases by imitating the teacher. As students advance, they can be exposed to phrases with more complicated rhythmic patterns and encouraged to create a complementary phrase to make a musical sentence. They can also sing, hum, and whistle tunes that vary in length according to their age group.

Students can sing or play melodies as they are written and then change them around. They can create new melodies and variations on them. As their experiences continue, they can create blues melodies using the standard AAB form. Use I–IV–V7 chords to harmonize these tunes. Discuss the blues scale and how it differs from the diatonic major scale. Students can sing and play the blues scale and become well-acquainted with the flatted 3rd, 5th, and 7th degrees of this scale. Notating the scale allows the students to have the visual as well as the aural experience.

Several students should be asked to sing the same melody in their own free personal interpretation, perhaps with body language. Discuss the differences between each rendition. When less complicated melodies are performed (homophonic texture), the accompanying instrumentalists can create polyrhythms. Encourage scat singing.

Experiences in harmony can include a recognition of the I–IV–V7 chords. Play examples of the blues and music of other countries that highlight these chords. Encourage students to demonstrate hearing these chords by raising the number of fingers that represent the chord being played. As students advance in age and grades, give them more complicated selections in which to identify musical components. For example, students might listen to recordings that have Middle Eastern, African, Cuban, and Brazilian influences. Students can hear and become familiar with the instruments, tonalities, and rhythms used in these different cultures. Use Miles Davis's "So What," for instance, to teach students how to count and listen to chord changes.

Many individuals derive great pleasure from listening to jazz. Even though they may lack the cognitive understanding, they appreciate the music for its aesthetic values. Where possible, films and videos of jazz concerts can be shown. Encourage students to be inquisitive about the social environment in which the music was performed. Linking music with the history and social mores of a people encourages and promotes critical thinking and stimulates creativity. This is essential in music education; students must learn to associate the contributions of various ethnic and cultural groups with the music they hear around them.

Jazz in Instrumental Music

The following outline is intended as a reference guide and is to be adjusted to the individual needs of the teacher or music program. It provides supplementary information and a practical guide to comprehensive jazz instrumental instruction.

The "Individual Performance and Listening Skills" section of this chapter shows individual skills applicable to each instrument. Several skills are common to all instruments, since playing jazz on any instrument uses the same basic fundamentals. Though it is possible to teach jazz education in heterogeneous groupings, many of the skills listed could be difficult to teach in such an environment.

The "Ensemble Performance and Listening Skills" section, while taught as individual instrumental skills, must also be presented in the context of ensemble skills. These skills should be introduced as early in the learning process as possible and continually reinforced throughout instrumental music study. Continued emphasis on these skills is the only way they can become second nature to the student.

The "Musical Concepts" and "Historical Information" sections complete this portion of the curriculum guide, offering a well-rounded perspective for the student's study.

Skills and Concepts
Recommended Performance Levels

Individual Performance and Listening Skills

Skill or Concept	Performance Level					
Basic Instrument Skills	**I**	**II**	**III**	**IV**	**V**	**VI**
Basic Vocalization	•	→	→	→	→	
Beginning Improvisation	•	→	→	→	→	
Articulation (Jazz Repertoire)	•	→	→	→	→	
Advanced Instrument Skills	**I**	**II**	**III**	**IV**	**V**	**VI**
Vocalization	•	→	→	→	→	
Improvisation		•	→	→	→	
Articulation (Jazz Repertoire)		•	→	→	→	
Vibrato			•	→	→	
Transposition			•	→	→	
Jazz Phrasing			•	→	→	
Specific Piano/Guitar/Bass Skills	**I**	**II**	**III**	**IV**	**V**	**VI**
Comping Techniques (Piano/Guitar)		•	→	→	→	
Electric Bass and Double String Bass		•	→	→	→	
Basic Jazz Voicings in Different Positions (Piano/Guitar)			•	→	→	
Learn Standard Chord Changes			•	→	→	
Learn Bass Styles (Walking Bass, etc.)			•	→	→	
Different Guitar Styles (Rock, Latin, Swing, etc.)			•	→	→	
Different Piano Styles (Boogie Woogie, Stride, etc.)					•	→
Specific Drum Set Skills	**I**	**II**	**III**	**IV**	**V**	**V**
Stick Control	•	→	→	→	→	
Simple Rhythms	•	→	→	→	→	
Pedal Techniques (Coordinated Independence)		•	→	→	→	
Hi-Hat, Brushes, Cymbals		•	→	→	→	
Complex Rhythms			•	→	→	

• = level at which skill or concept is normally introduced. (When more then one • appears, the skill or concept can be introduced at either level.)

→ = level at which skill or concept is normally reinforced.

Ensemble Performance and Listening Skills

Skills	I	II	III	IV	V	VI
Vocalization	•	→	→	→	→	
Improvisation	•	→	→	→	→	
Articulation/Phrasing (Jazz Literature)		•	→	→	→	

Pulse/Beat	I	II	III	IV	V	VI
Vocalization	•	→	→	→	→	
Measurement of Silence (Rests)	•	→	→	→	→	
Improvisation	•	→	→	→	→	
Flexibility (Rall., Accel., Rubato, etc.)		•	→	→	→	
Jazz Phrasing			•	→	→	

Intervals	I	II	III	IV	V	VI
Diatonic (M2, Me, P4, P5, M6, M7, P8va)	•	→	→	→	→	
Chromatic (m2, m3, A4/d5, m7)		•	→	→	→	
Enharmonic and Other Augmented/Diminished			•	→	→	

Musical Concepts—Rhythm

Rhythmic Notation/Stylistic Devices	I	II	III	IV	V	VI
Playing on downbeat, on upbeat	•	→	→	→	→	
Syncopation (e.g., eighth-quarter-eighth) (♪ ♩ ♪)		•	→	→	→	
Swinging Eighth Notes (e.g., quarter-eighth) (♩ ♪)		•	→	→	→	
Triplets		•	→	→	→	
Divisions and Subdivisions		•	→	→	→	
Reading Chord Symbols		•	→	→	→	
Blues, Swing, Shuffle, Rock, Ballad, Fanfare		•	→	→	→	
Playing Ahead of or Behind the Beat			•	→	→	
Jazz Articulations			•	→	→	
Specific Jazz Notations			•	→	→	
Latin Rock, Samba, Jazz Waltz			•	→	→	

Musical Concepts—Melody

Key Signatures and Scales (concert pitch)	**I**	**II**	**III**	**IV**	**V**	**VI**
Major Keys, Key of C through 4 sharps and 4 flats		•	→	→	→	
Chromatic Scale		•	→	→	→	
Blues Scale		•	→	→	→	
Modal Scales (e.g., Dorian, Mixolydian, etc.)		•	→	→	→	
Minor Keys, Key of Am through 4 sharps and 4 flats (natural form)			•	→	→	
Remaining Major Keys					•	→
Remaining Minor Keys					•	→
Whole-Tone Scales						•
Diminished Scales (half-whole and whole-half)						•
Half-diminished Scales						•

Melodic Notation/Terminology	**I**	**II**	**III**	**IV**	**V**	**VI**
Jazz Nomenclature			•	→	→	
Nontraditional Notation Systems					•	→

Musical Concepts—Harmony

Chords	**I**	**II**	**III**	**IV**	**V**	**VI**
Major Minor	•	→	→	→	→	
Dominant 7th/Major 7th/Minor 7th	•	→	→	→	→	
Jazz Nomenclature	•	→	→	→	→	
Diminished/Augmented		•	→	→	→	
Expanded Chords (e.g., 9ths, 11ths, 13ths)				•	→	
Tonal Clusters				•	→	
Flatted 5th and Other Altered Chords					•	→

Other Harmonic Concepts	**I**	**II**	**III**	**IV**	**V**	**VI**
Dissonance/Consonance	•	→	→	→	→	
Overtone Series/Harmonic Series		•	→	→	→	
Harmonic Progression, Harmonic Rhythm, Modulation, Voicings			•	→	→	

Musical Concepts—Form

Composition Devices	**I**	**II**	**III**	**IV**	**V**	**VI**
Repetition/Contrast, Section, Introduction, Coda, Blues	•	→	→	→	→	
Countermelody, Counterpoint, Augmentation		•	→	→	→	
Compositional Structures						
12 Bar Blues	•	→	→	→	→	
32 Bar AABA			•	→	→	
32 Bar ABAC			•	→	→	

Musical Concepts—Timbre/Texture

Effects	I	II	III	IV	V	VI
Vibrato (Diaphragm, Jaw, Hand)			•	→	→	
Fall, Smear (Other Jazz Effects)			•	→	→	
Muting		•	→	→	→	
Special Instrumental Techniques (Growl, Flutter Tongue, etc.)				•	→	→

Musical Concepts—Expression

Articulation	I	II	III	IV	V	VI
Slur, Staccato	•	→	→	→	→	
Accent, Legato, Detachment		•	→	→	→	
Other Jazz Articulation (Double Tongue, Offbeat Accent, Ghosting, etc.)			•	→	→	
Releases			•	→	→	

Historical Information

Stylistic Periods of Jazz	I	II	III	IV	V	VI
Early Jazz	•	→	→	→	→	
Modal	•	→	→	→	→	
Fusion		•	→	→	→	
Swing			•	→	→	
Bebop				•	→	
Cool				•	→	
Third Stream					•	→
Free Jazz						•

Specific String Skills	I	II	III	IV	V	VI
Swing Phrasing Techniques: Articulation (Bow Attack, Bowing Patterns, Combining Short Slurs in All Parts of Bow)			•	→	→	
Slurring across the Beat			•	→	→	
Double Stops			•	→	→	
Percussive Effects ("Chops," etc.)			•	→	→	
Ghost-Note Bowings and Fingerings				•	→	
Shakes (Vibrato by Glissando)				•	→	
Blues Slides (Glissando)				•	→	
Alternate Fingerings: Chromatic Scale				•	→	
Varying Finger Pressure and Vibrato for Different Sound Qualities				•	→	
Cello: Bass Styles (Walking, etc.)				•	→	
Comping Skills (Chords, Guide-Tones)					•	→
Different Jazz Styles (Latin/Jazz/Rock)					•	→

Jazz in Vocal Music

The placement here—toward the end of this guide—of information specific to vocal jazz is not any reflection on its importance. Indeed, careful readers will have noted by now *repeated* emphasis on vocal improvisation skills for instrumentalists, as well as continued exposure to the vocal jazz masters. This section appears where it does because it is the consensus of vocal jazz educators that much common ground is shared between vocal and instrumental jazz. For this reason, teachers of both genres should examine this guide in full—not merely looking for assistance within their most familiar territory. The "Scope and Sequence" chart illustrates a wealth of experiences that should be part of quality jazz instruction for all students; the final category, "Vocal Skills," lists initiatives that are more indigenous to the vocal jazz track. These are the points focused upon in this portion of the guide.

The more simple jazz standards can be sung at very early ages and experience levels. By using both aural and written music, students should be encouraged to sing with good tone (in imitation of the teacher). Specific instruction on basic tone-production techniques is often best left for a somewhat later time so these details do not distract from simple imitation. Gradually students should explore these techniques, such as proper breathing, diction, color of the tone, and more. Most of the singing can take place in unison groups, with gradual attention toward achieving an appropriate level of blend and balance.

As students' experience and exposure grows, teachers can introduce a basic vocabulary of sounds for scatting: the vowels oo and ah, consonants b, d, m, n, and v. Though they will already be exposed to call and response (see "Ear Training"), students can explore basic solo singing and the beginning of singing parts within a vocal group. Using the simple tunes already introduced, students should sing the chord roots of the tunes and of other basic chord progressions (I–IV–V–I, ii–V–I, iii–VI–ii–V–I) by employing intervallic recognition (often tied to phrases of tunes known well by the students). Introduce new repertoire regularly. As with all improvisers, emphasize motivic development in improvisation.

A concern more specific to vocalists is proper microphone technique, for the mike becomes an extension of the voice and part of the instrument. Teachers should demonstrate good technique to the students and monitor their progress.

Level III examines the issue of breaks in the voice register. Each student should learn where his or her voice shifts registers, and teachers should assist with exercises to smooth over those breaks. Men have the additional color of falsetto to explore and cultivate. As experience grows, students' warm-ups should also grow to be less group-oriented and more personalized.

Students can bring ear training to life by singing roots and thirds of simple tunes and progressions. As they learn new repertoire, increased focus on appropriate style should be apparent. With the growth of the vocal instrument, students should discuss the quality of their resonance while retaining the tone color. Teachers can also introduce new stimuli for vocal imitation: drum sounds, growls, other musical instruments, and more.

As students enter the environment of working with a rhythm section, a new interplay must develop. Vocalists must learn how to communicate effectively with the rhythm players (and vice-versa). This includes the ability to write lead sheets and transpose keys as well as to discuss the role of each member of the ensemble. The constant exposure to recorded examples of jazz should include an aggressive effort to identify, define, and request properly the various rhythmic "grooves" inherent to typical styles: swing, shuffle, two- or four-feel, jazz waltz, bossa, samba, and more.

Level IV calls for an analysis of basic physiology related to vocal sound production. By learning how their voices work—and the forces that irritate them—students can develop the motivation to adopt behavior patterns that will promote good vocal health. Natural vibrato, a reflex action that assists in protecting the vocal cords, should be cultivated into a controllable artistic expression.

Students should now be ready to sing full arpeggios of chords within tunes and appropriate chord progressions (such as I–VI–ii–V). In conjunction with their keyboard instruction, students should be able to play chord roots on the piano while singing a solo or written part. As always, continue to expand the repertoire of tunes learned—with attention to style, mike technique, blend, balance, and other considerations already introduced.

The students' sense of proper style for a given tune should grow strongly with each exposure. By Level V, previous experience singing roots and arpeggios of chord progressions—coupled with constant exposure to styles—should grow into an increasing facility singing bass lines to tunes and progressions. Previously learned arpeggios can now proceed through the cycle of fifths or half steps to promote readiness in all keys. And continued partnership with the rhythm section leads to a greater understanding of individual needs and shared goals so that the rapport already in place strengthens.

Level VI calls for the students to accompany their singing at the piano. (The given "Jazz Keyboard" skills introduced earlier should provide the vocalist with a functional level of piano skills.) Ensemble singing can split into advanced four- to eight-part groups. Most important, this is a time for greater exposure and attention to the vast styles and techniques already introduced that enhance the musical quality of any jazz musician.

The Sound Reinforcement System in Vocal Jazz

When you see a vocal jazz ensemble perform for the first time what may strike you is the array of microphones and speakers. This is how vocal jazz is performed: on a sound system. Though some people have philosophical problems with miking the choir, be assured the system does not correct musical elements; it merely amplifies and supports the nuance of the idiom. The microphone and all else between vocalist and listener are part of the vocal jazz performer's instrument. Train your singers to produce tone with freedom, flow, ring, and roundness—off the system and on. Five elements make up the sound system: the microphone, mixer, amplifier, speakers, and monitors.

Microphone

The ideal in vocal jazz is one person per mike. There are many acceptable microphones available. The best microphone for vocal jazz is a low-impedance vocal microphone with a cardioid (heart-shaped) pick-up pattern. Do not buy microphones or any other sound equipment at a "stereo store." Go to a reputable audio equipment dealer.

Mixer

This piece of equipment is designed to mix all the inputs and generate mono or stereo sound. Mixers come either with or without an integrated amplifier. If the amplifier is integrated, there is less equipment, although this adds considerable weight. The technology is advancing so rapidly that a twelve- or sixteen-channel powered (integrated mixer-amplifier) board weighs significantly less than the integrated boards of five years ago. The newer boards are very efficient and dependable. Each channel on the mixer has separate controls for attenuation (adjusting the microphone sensitivity), reverberation, bass equalization, mid-range equalization, treble equalization, monitor send, and house speaker volume. The equalizing sound control allows the sound technician to match as closely as possible the voice on the system with the natural acoustic sound of an individual voice. On most mixers, the monitor sound the choir hears is not equalized. The monitor send will also need a separate amplifier, as the majority of integrated amplifiers do not have an integrated monitor amplifier. The other controls on the mixer affect the mixed sound going out through the house speakers. The sound person and mixer need to be set up in the center of the audience rather than off to the side of the stage. The microphone signal travels to the mixer via a "snake." This is usually a sixteen- or twenty-five-channel extension cord. The microphones plug into one end, and the signal is carried back to the mixing board where individual connections are made.

Amplifier

If you are not using a mixer with an integrated amplifier, you must purchase a separate amplifier. The amplifier usually has two inputs and two outputs. The signal from the mixer is routed to the input, and the speakers are connected to the outputs. Generally, an amplifier is designed to drive two speakers or two monitors: the absolute minimum for any system. Thus two amplifiers may be required. Amplifiers send a certain number of "watts" per channel. For optimal sound quality, seek more watts per channel; there will be less potential sound distortion as the higher-wattage amplifiers will run more efficiently and will not have to be turned up as much as the lower-wattage amplifiers. There are many possibilities; check with your dealer or retailer or both.

The signal sent to the monitors and speakers needs to be equalized before it is amplified. Equalizing adjusts certain band-width responses to compensate for the acoustics of the room in which the ensemble is performing. Many mixing boards include seven- to ten-band equalizers (generally referred to simply as EQ). Each fader on the EQ can boost or decrease a certain range of frequency response. The ideal sound is the most natural, closest to the acoustic sound of the ensemble. However, in many cases, the performance venue will dictate a somewhat different equalization to prevent feedback. Feedback occurs when a frequency is looped through the system (mike to speaker to mike, etc.) and sounds like a static pitch, usually of ever-increasing volume.

Speakers

You will need a full-range speaker that gives good response over the entire range of the human voice. At the minimum, the cabinet should have a ten-inch or twelve-inch speaker, one to four eight-inch speakers, and a horn (tweeter) for the high frequencies to add the shimmer of the upper sympathetic harmonics. The speakers can be bought as separate components: a bass cabinet, a mid-range cabinet, and a tweeter cabinet. A good alternative to the large cabinets and individual components is the mini-public-address speaker.

Monitors

Monitors are speakers designed for the performers to hear what they are producing. Monitors are extremely important in vocal jazz. The singers must hear the balance, blend, stylistic nuance, and intonation before making immediate adjustments. Good mixers will have separate volume controls and outputs for monitors and speakers.

Purchasing Equipment

Quality is always a concern, and there are some consistent product lines. Consider the following names when you are buying:

Microphone	Shure SM-58, Sennheiser Black Fire 501, Audio Technica ATM 41a
Microphone stand	Shure MS 10-C, Atlas, Borg
Mixer	Audio Pro, Mackie, Peavey, Ramsa, Soundcraft, Yamaha
Amplifier	Carver, Crate, Electro Voice, Peavey, QSC, Traynor, Yamaha, Yorkville
Speakers	Bose, Yamaha, Yorkville, Elite, Meyer, JBL, Electro Voice, MacPherson
Monitor	Yamaha, Bose, Yorkville, Elite, ElectroVoice, Meyer.

This is by no means a complete listing of possible equipment. The director's best friend may well be the support staff of a reputable audio equipment dealer. Use the above names for comparative purposes of quality and cost.

For some reason, cost often seems to be more of a factor when considering a vocal program rather than an instrumental program. The sound system does not come cheaply. Look upon its acquisition as an investment in quality, diversified education. If the original expenditure looks overwhelming, think in terms of a three-to-four-year acquisition and building program. If you start out with the basic equipment, the students will love the sound system and want to upgrade—perhaps even with their fund-raising assistance. Consider the alternative: a good ensemble heard over a mediocre sound system will sound mediocre. That would be unfair to them and to you, and lessen the ensemble's chances for success. Look for support from teachers who are already involved in vocal jazz, from suppliers and retailers who know the idiom, institutions that have successful vocal jazz programs, and the IAJE.

A Selected List of Sound Reinforcement Books

Davis, Gary, and Ralph Jones. *Sound Reinforcement Handbook.* 2nd ed. Milwaukee: Hal Leonard Publishing, 1988.

Microphone Techniques for Music. Evanston, IL: Shure Brother, Inc., 1994.

The PA Bible. Buchanan, MI: Electro-Voice, Inc., 1991.

Resources for Jazz Education

The materials listed represent a wealth of resources now available to educators and students. This list is not intended to be all-inclusive. Many excellent resources have been omitted and more are published each year.

IAJE encourages the reader to refer to current and previous issues of its *Jazz Educators Journal* for a constant and more thorough perspective of resources. Virtually each issue includes audio, video, software, hardware, text, and other reviews. A compilation of hundreds of annotated reviews of instructional materials is available from IAJE.

In addition, the annual conference provides hands-on opportunities to experience these jazz resources. Finally, the network of IAJE state and regional officers can assist you and your colleagues in your efforts to find the most appropriate teaching tools.

Jazz Pedagogy Resources

Aebersold, Jamey. *A New Approach to Improvisation* (Multiple Volumes). Jamey Aebersold, 1972–1996.

Anderson, Douglas. *The Jazz and Showchoir Handbook II.* Chapel Hill, NC: Hinshaw Music, Inc., 1993.

Anschell, Bill. *Who Can I Turn To? A Guide to Jazz Funding Programs.* Atlanta, GA: Southern Arts Federation, 1994.

Baker, David. *Jazz Pedagogy.* Los Angeles, CA: Alfred Music, 1988.

Berliner, Paul. *Thinking in Jazz.* Chicago: University of Chicago Press, 1994.

Coker, Jerry. *Improvising Jazz.* New York: Simon and Schuster, 1987.

Coker, Jerry. *The Teaching of Jazz.* Rottenburg, Germany: Advance Music, 1989.

Dunscomb, Marcia. *Melody Maker, Vol. 1.* Hollywood, FL: Melody Maker Press, 1991.

Haerle, Dan. *The Jazz Language.* Miami: Studio PR, 1980.

Hill, Willie, and Bob Montgomery. *Sight Reading and the Jazz Idiom.* New York: Ardsley Publishing, 1994.

Houghton, Steve. *A Guide for the Modern Rhythm Section.* Oskaloosa, IA: Barnhouse Publishing, 1978.

Kuzmich, John, and Lee Bash. *Complete Guide to Instrumental Jazz Instruction.* Miami: CPP Belwin, 1992.

Lawn, Rick. *The Jazz Ensemble Director's Manual.* Oskaloosa, IA: Barnhouse Publishing, 1986.

Levine, Mark. *The Jazz Piano Book.* Petaluma, CA: Sher Music, 1989.

Malabe, Frank, and Bob Weiner. *Afro-Cuban Rhythms for the Drumset.* Miami: CPP Belwin, 1990.

Mantooth, Frank. *Voicings for Jazz Piano.* Milwaukee, WI: Hal Leonard Publishing, 1986.

Mauleón, Rebecca. *Salsa Guidebook for Piano & Ensemble.* Petaluma, CA: Sher Music, 1993.

Meadows, Eddie. *Jazz Reference and Research Materials.* New York: Garland Publishing, 1981.

Megill and Demory. *Introduction to Jazz History.* Englewood Cliffs, NJ: Prentice Hall, 1996.

Raph, Alan. *Dance Band Reading and Interpretation.* Ft. Lauderdale, FL: Sam Fox Publishing, 1962.

Shaw, Kirby. *Junior Jazz: Beginning Steps to Singing Jazz.* Milwaukee, WI: Hal Leonard Publishing, 1993; reprint, 1995.

Shaw, Kirby. *Vocal Jazz Style.* 2nd ed. Milwaukee, WI: Hal Leonard Publishing, 1987; reprint, 1995.

Shaw, Kirby. *Vocal Jazz Warmups.* Greeley, CO: UNC Jazz Press, 1990.

Williams, Martin, and Gunther Schuller, eds. *Big Band Jazz.* Washington, DC: Smithsonian Institution, 1983.

Williams, Martin. *Jazz Piano.*Washington, DC: Smithsonian Institution, 1987.

Williams, Martin. *The Smithsonian Collection of Jazz.* Washington, DC: Smithsonian Institution, 1987.

Jazz Journals and Periodicals

Coda Magazine
Box 87, Station J
Toronto, Ontario M4J 4X8 Canada

Down Beat Magazine
P.O. Box 906
Elmhurst, IL 60126-0906

Jazz Educators Journal
International Association of Jazz Educators
P.O. Box 724
Manhattan, KS 66502

Jazziz
3620 NW 43rd St.
Gainesville, FL 32606

Jazz Player
Dorn Publications, Inc.
P.O. Box 206
Medfield, MA 02052

Jazz Times
7961 Eastern Ave., Suite 303
Silver Spring, MD 20910-4898

NAJE Educator and Jazz Educators Journal Index
1969-1989
Lee Bash, Ed.
P.O. Box 724
Manhattan, KS 66505

Windplayer
P.O. Box 15753
North Hollywood, CA 91615-9913

General Music Education Journals

Music Educators Journal
1806 Robert Fulton Drive
Reston, VA 20191-4348

Teaching Music
1806 Robert Fulton Drive
Reston, VA 20191-4348

The Instrumentalist
200 Northfield Rd.
Northfield, IL 60093

A Selected List of Jazz History Texts

Berendt, Joachim. *The Jazz Book.* 6th ed. Brooklyn, NY: Lawrence Hill Books, 1992.

Carner, Gary, Ed. *Jazz Performers.* Westport, CT: Greenwood Press, 1990.

Collier, James Lincoln. *The Making of Jazz.* New York: Delta Books, 1978.

Feather, Leonard. *The Book of Jazz.* New York: Meridan Books, 1959.

Gridley, Mark. *Jazz Styles.* 5th ed. Engelwood Cliffs, NJ: Prentice Hall, 1993.

Nanry, Charles and Edward Berger. *The Jazz Text.* New York: D. Van Nostrand Co., 1979.

Ostransky, Leroy. *Jazz City.* Engelwood Cliffs, NJ: Prentice Hall, 1978.

Ostransky, Leroy. *Understanding Jazz.* Engelwood Cliffs, NJ: Prentice Hall, 1977.

Sales, Grover. *Jazz; America's Classical Music.* New York: Da Capo Press, 1992.

Schuller, Gunther. *Early Jazz.* New York: Oxford University Press, 1968.

Schuller, Gunther. *The Swing Era.* New York: Oxford University Press, 1989.

Stearns, Marshall. *The Story of Jazz.* New York: Oxford University Press, 1977.

Tanner, Paul, Maurice Gerow, and David Megill. *A Study of Jazz.* Dubuque, IA: WC Brown Publishing, 1992.

Tirro, Frank. *Jazz: A History.* New York: W.W. Norton & Co., 1992.

A Selected List of Jazz Standard Tunes

The following graded list of jazz standards represents an essential repertoire for jazz students. These selections are available in the indicated volume of *A New Approach to Jazz Improvisation* by Jamey Aebersold. The Ricker selection is available in *The Beginning Improvisor* by Ramon Ricker.

Easy

(Blues, modal, and simple ii–V standards)

"Billie's Bounce"	Vol. 6 AEB
"Blue Bossa"	Vol. 54 AEB
"Cantaloupe Island"	Vol. 11 AEB
"Don't Get Around"	Vol. 48 AEB
"Doxy"	Vol. 54 AEB
"Footprints"	Vol. 54 AEB
"Impressions"	Vol. 54 AEB
"In a Mellow Tone"	Vol. 48 AEB
"Ladybird"	Vol. 36 AEB
"Little Sunflower"	Vol. 60 AEB
"Maiden Voyage"	Vol. 54 AEB
"Now's the Time"	Vol. 6 AEB
"Sandu"	Vol. 53 AEB
"Satin Doll"	Vol. 54 AEB
"So What"	Vol. 50 AEB
"Song for My Father"	Vol. 54 AEB
"St. Thomas"	Vol. 8 AEB
"Summer Time"	Vol. 25, 54 AEB
"Take the A Train"	Vol. 12 AEB
"Tune Up"	Vol. 7 AEB
"Watch What Happens"	Vol. 55 AEB
"Watermelon Man"	Vol. 11 AEB

Medium

(Longer forms, minor ii–V, and ballads)

"Another You"	Vol. 15 AEB
"Autumn Leaves"	Vol. 54 AEB
"Days of Wine and Roses"	Vol. 40 AEB
"Four"	Vol. 7 AEB
"Freddie Freeloader"	Vol. 50 AEB
"Green Dolphin Street"	Vol. 34 AEB
"I Mean You"	Vol. 56 AEB
"Just Friends"	Vol. 34 AEB
"Mr. P. C."	Vol. 27 AEB
"My Shining Hour"	Vol. 44 AEB
"My Funny Valentine"	Vol. 25 AEB

"Oleo"	Vol. 8 AEB
"Ornithology"	Vol. 6 AEB
"Shadow of Your Smile"	Vol. 34 AEB
"Soft as in a Morning Sunrise"	Vol. 40 AEB
"Solar"	Vol. 47 AEB
"Straight No Chaser"	Vol. 2 AEB
"Yardbird Suite"	Vol. 6 AEB
"Yesterdays"	Vol. 5 Ricker

Medium / Advanced

(Altered chords and chord cycles)

"All the Things You Are"	Vol. 43 AEB
"Bluesette"	Vol. 43 AEB
"Body and Soul"	Vol. 41 AEB
"Confirmation"	Vol. 6 AEB
"Donna Lee"	Vol. 6 AEB
"The Girl from Ipanema"	Vol. 31 AEB
"Have You Met Miss Jones"	Vol. 25 AEB
"Here's That Rainy Day"	Vol. 23 AEB
"Joy Spring"	Vol. 53 AEB
"Misty"	Vol. 49 AEB
"My Favorite Things"	Vol. 25 AEB
"Nica's Dream"	Vol. 18 AEB
"Night in Tunisia"	Vol. 43 AEB
"Quiet Nights"	Vol. 31 AEB
"Secret Love"	Vol. 34 AEB
"Speak Low"	Vol. 25 AEB
"Stella by Starlight"	Vol. 15 AEB
"There Is No Greater Love"	Vol. 34 AEB
"The Way You Look Tonight"	Vol. 55 AEB
"Wave"	Vol. 31 AEB
"Well You Needn't"	Vol. 56 AEB
"You Stepped out of a Dream"	Vol. 34 AEB

Advanced

"Along Came Betty"	Vol. 28 AEB
"Cherokee"	Vol. 15 AEB
"Dolphin Dance"	Vol. 11 AEB
"Giant Steps"	Vol. 28 AEB
"Invitation"	Vol. 34 AEB
"One Note Samba"	Vol. 31 AEB
"'Round Midnight"	Vol. 56 AEB
"Stablemates"	Vol. 14 AEB

A Selected List of Jazz Band Arrangements

A starter jazz band library is based on educational and performance needs of the program as the director perceives them. The ability level of the students must be considered when purchasing arrangements, and for this reason comments have been inserted for each grade level. A definition of grade levels follows:

Grade 2: Junior High or Middle School

Grade 3: Advanced Junior High/High School

Grade 4: High School

Grade 5: Advanced High School/College

Within each grade level, charts are selected in four categories:

(1) Swing-Shuffle

(2) Ballad

(3) Latin, Rock, or other eighth-note selection

(4) Special—refers to anything from an educational aid to a chart that may serve as an encore or add "spice" to a program.

Recorded examples of the charts are important so students hear the music played properly. When possible, prepare tapes of the charts for student listening.

At the end of this section is a listing of most major publishers of jazz arrangements and related jazz material. It is strongly suggested that the director write to these companies and request to be placed on their mailing list. Many of these publishers also include preview tapes that are helpful when assessing the level and appropriateness of the material.

Grade 2

This grade level should emphasize "educational" material—both in theory and practice. Therefore, these selections focus on basic "swing-teaching" arrangements. The Latin-rock charts are primarily those that take the student's current level of musical interest and use it as a bridge to swing-style jazz. The "educational" pieces are used primarily for warm-up exercises at the start of each rehearsal.

Swing-Shuffle, Grade 2

Composer/Arranger	Name of Selection	Publisher
Beach-Shutack	"The Flash"	Beach/Kjos
Chattaway, Jay	"Just a Little Off the Top"	Wm. Allen
Chattaway, Jay	"Swing Shift"	Wm. Allen
Edmondson, Paul	"Blues for Mr. B"	Hal Leonard
Ellington/Edmondson	"Satin Doll"	Hal Leonard
Ellington/Lowden	"Take the A Train"	Hal Leonard
Feldstein, Sandy	"Big Bad Bill"	CPP/Belwin
Gingery, Ralph	"Blues for Bart"	Wm. Allen
Harris, Matt	"Snooze, You Lose"	Kendor
Niehaus, Lennie	"Best Bet"	Barnhouse
Sweeney, Mike	"Killer Joe"	Hal Leonard
Taylor, Mark	"601 Blues"	Jenson/Leonard

Taylor, Jeff	"That's a Wrap"	Wm. Allen
Taylor, Jeff	"Why Not?"	Wm. Allen
Taylor, Jeff	"Headlines"	Wm. Allen
Taylor, Jeff	"Kicks"	Wm. Allen

Ballad, Grade 2

Beach-Shutack	"A Little More Time"	Beach/Kjos
Carmichael/Taylor	"Georgia on My Mind"	Jenson
Chattaway, Jay	"Mystery Woman"	Wm. Allen
Hefti, Neal	"Li'l Darlin'"	Jenson
Nestico, Sammy	"Crystal"	Hal Leonard
Taylor, Jeff	"Quiet Time"	Wm. Allen
Yasinitsky, Greg	"For My Dad"	Kendor

Latin-Rock, Grade 2

Beach-Shutack	"Paso Robles"	Beach/Kjos
Chattaway, Jay	"Drive Time"	Wm. Allen
Gingery, Ralph	"Castles of Sand"	Wm. Allen
Gingery, Ralph	"Cordova"	Wm. Allen
Gingery, Ralph	"Ocean View"	Wm. Allen
Taylor, Jeff	"Salsa Nueva"	Wm. Allen

Special, Grade 2

Beach, Doug	"Swing Rhythms"	Beach
Clark, Andy	"Tin Roof Blues"	Hal Leonard
DiBlasio, Dennis	*Jazz Ensemble Book*	Kendor
Lewis-Bullock	*Warm-up Exercises*	CPP/Belwin
Nestico, Sammy	*The Best of Sammy Nestico*	Hal Leonard
Spera, Dominic	*Gospel According to Miles*	Barnhouse

Grade 3

Most beginning jazz teaching occurs in high school at this level. The emphasis continues to be in the swing-shuffle category.

Swing-Shuffle, Grade 3

Composer/Arranger	Name of Selection	Publisher
Barduhn, Dave, arr.	"Take the A Train"	Jenson
Barduhn, Dave, arr.	"So What"	Jenson
Barduhn, Dave, arr.	"Groove"	Merchant
Blair, Peter, arr.	"Four Brothers"	Hal Leonard
Carubia, Mike	"Brushes Anyone?"	CPP/Belwin

Fedchock, John	"Blues Over Easy"	Kendor
Goodwin, Gordon, arr.	"Lester Leaps In"	Warner Bros.
Goodwin, Gordon, arr.	"Beginning to See Light"	Hal Leonard
Harris, Matt	"Mattitude"	Kendor
Harris, Matt	"Blue Basket"	Kendor
Holmes, Roger, arr.	"Fever"	Hal Leonard
Jennings, Paul, arr.	"Stolen Moments"	Jenson
Mantooth, Frank	"Trickle down Shuffle"	Kendor
Matteson, Rich	"Doo, Dit Dot"	CPP/Belwin
Mintzer, Bob	"Easy Street"	Kendor
Mintzer, Bob	"Nice'n' Easy Blues"	Kendor
Nestico, Sammy, arr.	"Alright, Okay You Win"	Hal Leonard
Nestico, Sammy	"Reachin' Out"	Kendor
Nestico, Sammy	"Count the Aces"	Jenson/Leonard
Nestico, Sammy	"Time Waits for No One"	Kendor
Nestico, Sammy, arr.	"Satin Doll"	Hal Leonard
Schneider, Maria	"Baytrail Shuffle"	Kendor
Schneider, Maria	"Salina"	Kendor
Schneider, Maria	"Smooth Talk"	Kendor
Schneider, Maria	"Swing Street"	Kendor
Spera, Dominic	"Blue Bones"	Barnhouse
Taylor, Mark, arr.	"Jumpin' at the Woodside"	Jenson/Leonard
Wolpe, Dave, arr.	"Just Friends"	CPP/Belwin

Ballad, Grade 3

Bellson-Black	"Crystals"	Barnhouse
Berry, John, arr.	"Misty"	Jenson
Carubia, Mike	"Tracy"	CPP/Belwin
Mantooth, Frank, arr.	"Harlem Nocturne"	Barnhouse
Metheny/Curnow, arr.	"Letter from Home"	Sierra
Taylor, Mark, arr.	"My Funny Valentine"	Jenson/Leonard
Taylor, Mark	"My One and Only Love"	Jenson/Leonard
Wolpe, Dave	"Round Midnight"	CPP/Belwin

Latin-Rock, Grade 3

Beach-Shutack	"No Peppers, No Tomatoes"	Beach/Kjos
Carubia, Mike	"Gary's Place"	CPP/Belwin
Davis, Miles	"Easy Minor"	Kendor
Harris, Matt	"Mr. Basket"	Kendor
Harris, Matt	"Blue Basket"	Kendor
Lopez, Victor	"Fudge Said the Judge"	Ed. Programs
Lopez, Victor	"Oye, Que Pasa"	Ed. Programs
Mantooth, Frank, arr.	"Fly Me to the Moon"	Barnhouse
Sabina, Les	"Selfish Shellfish"	Kendor

Special, Grade 3

Beach-Shutack	*Rock Rhythms*	Beach/Kjos
Beach-Shutack	*Swing Rhythms*	Beach/Kjos
DiBlasio, Dennis	*Jazz Ensemble Book*	Kendor
Goodwin, Gordon, arr.	"Good King Wenceslas"	Hal Leonard
Holmes, Roger, arr.	"Mr. Bojangles"	Hal Leonard
Nestico, Sammy	*The Best of Sammy Nestico*	Hal Leonard

Grade 4

At this level, the library should contain more charts related to jazz classics. The charts on this list requiring the most effort are those with historical significance. Students at this level should be ready to appreciate the quality of material they are performing.

Swing-Shuffle, Grade 4

Composer/Arranger	Name of Selection	Publisher
Beal, Jeff	"A Blues Grows in Brooklyn"	CPP/Belwin
Berger, Dave, arr.	"Corner Pocket"	Jenson/Leonard
Berger, Dave, arr.	"Take the A Train"	Jenson/Leonard
Berry, John, arr.	"Seven Steps to Heaven"	Jenson/Leonard
Blair, Peter, arr.	"Blue Birdland"	Hal Leonard
Caffey, Dave	"Murphy Strut"	Kendor
Dilkey, John	"The Rufus Shuffle"	Ed. Programs
Hefti, Neal	"Cute"	Jenson/Leonard
Hooper, Les	"Pulling Punches"	Barnhouse
Keezer, Geoff, arr.	"Dragon Blues"	Sierra
Keezer, Geoff, arr.	"Work Song"	Sierra
Kubis,Tom, arr.	"When You're Smiling"	Walrus
Kubis, Tom	"Exactly like This"	Walrus
Menza/Barduhn, arr.	"Groovin' Hard"	Jenson/Leonard
Mintzer, Bob	"Life of the Party"	Kendor
Morey, Brad, arr.	"Prelude to a Kiss"	Warner Bros.
Morey, Brad, arr.	"Summertime"	Warner Bros.
Nestico, Sammy	"Travelin' Home"	Barnhouse
Nestico, Sammy	"Freckle Face"	Kendor
Nestico, Sammy	"Hay Burner"	Kendor
Nestico, Sammy	"Take One"	Jenson Leonard
Nestico, Sammy	"Basie Straight Ahead"	Kendor
Nestico, Sammy, arr.	"A Night in Tunisia"	Hal Leonard
Niehaus, Lennie, arr.	"Moose the Mooche"	Barnhouse
Taylor, Mark, arr.	"Maiden Voyage"	Jenson
Taylor, Mark, arr.	"Dat Dere"	Jenson/Leonard

Wolpe, Dave, arr.	"Cottontail"	CPP/Belwin
Wolpe, Dave, arr.	"C Jam Blues"	CPP/Belwin
Wolpe, Dave, arr.	"Take Five"	CPP/Belwin
Wolpe, Dave, arr.	"Caravan"	CPP/Belwin

Ballad, Grade 4

Higgins-Taylor, arr.	"'Round Midnight"	Jenson/Leonard
Jennings, Paul, arr.	"Stolen Moments"	Jenson/Leonard
Kubis, Tom, arr.	"The Nearness of You"	Walrus
Mantooth, Frank, arr.	"Spring Can Really Hang You Up"	Kendor
Mendelson, Manny, arr.	"Naima"	Kendor
Nestico, Sammy, arr.	"God Bless the Child"	Hal Leonard
Nestico, Sammy, arr.	"Lover Man"	Jenson/Leonard
Nestico, Sammy, arr.	"Georgia on My Mind"	Jenson/Leonard
Nestico, Sammy, arr.	"I Remember Clifford"	Jenson/Leonard
Taylor, Mark, arr.	"My Romance"	Hal Leonard

Latin-Rock, Grade 4

Berg, Shelly	"Man Tuna"	Lou Fischer
Carney, Gary	"Flying High"	Hal Leonard
Fedchock, John	"Louie's Cheese Party"	Kendor
Goodwin, Gordon	"Sao Paulo"	Hal Leonard
Harris, Matt	"Mira Mira"	Kendor
Harris, Matt	"Shmoozability"	Kendor
Hooper, Les	"Juan of These Days"	Jenson
Jarvis, Jeff	"Power to Spare"	Kendor
Lopez, Victor	"You Snooze, You Lose"	Ed. Programs
Tomaro, Mike	"Sweet Sorrow"	Lou Fischer

Special, Grade 4

Beach-Shutack	Rock Rhythms	Beach/Kjos
Beach-Shutack	Swing Rhythms	Beach/Kjos
Beach, Doug	"Ten Gallon Hat"	Beach/Kjos
Berg, Shelly	"Takin' It to Church"	Kendor
Hooper, Les, arr.	"Alexander's Ragtime Band"	Jenson/Leonard
Hooper, Les, arr.	"Down by the Riverside"	Jenson/Leonard
Lindsay, Gary	"New Orleans March"	CPP/Belwin

Grade 5

There is excellent material at this grade level that can be very challenging. Much important historical material is available as transcriptions. Saxophonists may be asked to double on other woodwinds, and trumpet players should have flugelhorns. The rhythm section parts may only indicate chord changes; so it is important that they know how to interpret the indicated chords. The contemporary Latin-rock styles will be more sophisticated and students may encounter arrangements in time meters other than 4/4 and 3/4.

Swing-Shuffle, Grade 5

Composer/Arranger	Name of Selection	Publisher
Beach, Doug	"Cut and Paste"	Doug Beach
Bellson/Mantooth, arr.	"How Sweets It Is"	Kendor
Brisker, Gordon	"Scat"	Kendor
Catingub, Matt	"Thadish"	Walrus
Catingub, Matt	"Stompin' at the Savoy"	UNC Jazz Press
Catingub, Matt	"I'm Getting Cement All over You"	Walrus
Dechter, Brad	"Hammy"	Lou Fischer
Ellington, Duke	"Koko"	King Brand
Ellington, Duke	"Cottontail"	King Brand
Foster, Frank	"Shiny Stockings"	Walrus
Harris, Matt	"Potato Blues"	Kendor
Horney, Al	"Hipper by the Dozen"	Beach/Kjos
Jones, Thad	"Three and One"	Kendor
Jones, Thad	"Kids Are Pretty People"	Kendor
Mantooth, Frank, arr.	"Mean to Me"	Jenson/Leonard
Mintzer, Bob	"Tribute"	Kendor
Mintzer, Bob	"Treasure Island"	Kendor
Mintzer, Bob, arr.	"But Not for Me"	Kendor
Nestico, Sammy, arr.	"Sweet Georgia Brown"	Hal Leonard
Nestico, Sammy	"Winner's Circle"	Jenson/Leonard
Pendowski, Mike	"Back at the Flat"	CPP/Belwin
Taylor, Mark, arr.	"Groovin' High"	Hal Leonard
Taylor, Mark, arr.	"The Song Is You"	Jenson/Leonard
Weimer, Andy	"Cruisin' for a Bluesin'"	Hal Leonard
Whitfield, Scott	"G'Day Mates"	UNC Jazz Press
Wright, Rayburn	"Sackbut City"	Kendor

Ballad, Grade 5

Fedchock, John	"Angel Eyes"	Kendor
Mantooth, Frank	"Stapes"	Barnhouse
Mantooth, Frank	"To a Forgotten Friend"	Wm. Allen

Mantooth, Frank, arr.	"You've Changed"	CPP/Belwin
Washut, Bob, arr.	"'Round Midnight"	UNC Jazz Press

Latin-Rock, Grade 5

Gailey, Dan	"Funk by Numbers"	UNC Jazz Press
Metheny/Lindsay, arr.	"Better Days Ahead"	Sierra
Meyer, Bobby	"Check Made"	CPP/Belwin
Mintzer, Bob	"Latin Dance"	Kendor
Mintzer, Bob	"Papa Lips"	Kendor
Stone, George	"Giant Steps"	UNC Press
Tomaro, Mike	"Dancing Eyes"	Beach/Kjos

A Selected List of Jazz Combo Arrangements

Incorporating jazz combos into a high school or college music program can be rewarding and beneficial. Because there are fewer students, much one-on-one teaching can take place. Jazz improvisation, theory, history, and performance are all stressed in the small group setting with more opportunity for students to improvise. When the question of suitable material arises, there are various avenues that may be explored.

There are published combo arrangements with flexible instrumentation for one to four horns and rhythm section for beginning through advanced levels. The *Combo Paks* are cost effective and easy to use because each one contains several compositions. Many individual arrangements are available for easy to advanced levels. There are original compositions and transcriptions from records (*Second Floor Music*). Arrangements are available through most of the publishing companies. A description and rating are included in the catalogs.

Another direction is to use legal fakebooks, of which there are many available. Students can begin to learn important jazz repertoire and write their own arrangements. Students using lead sheets should be able to read chord changes, realize voicings on piano or guitar, and walk bass lines. This takes more time, but the students will derive greater benefit. Students should also be encouraged (or required) to bring original compositions to rehearsal.

Jazz Combo Paks, #1–26
Edited By Frank Mantooth and Roger Pemberton
Hal Leonard Music

Jazz Combo Rehearsal Guidelines
Jamey Aebersold Music

Second Floor Music
Edited by Don Sickler
Originals and "Blue Note" Transcriptions

Various Combinations

Title	Publisher	Composer	Arranger	Grade	Type/Feel
"All The Things You Are"	Kendor Music	Hammerstein/Kern	Lennie Niehaus	4 1/2	Swing
"Dancing Bishop"	Neil Kjos	Bobby Shew	Bobby Shew	5	Latin
"Desafinado"	Kendor Music	Carlos Jobim	Matt Harris	3	Bossa Nova
"Kyss Abyss"	Neil Kjos	Bobby Shew	Bobby Shew	4 1/2	Latin
"Maiden Voyage"	Hal Leonard	Herbie Hancock	Roger Pemberton	4	Latin
"Mann Oh Mann"	UNC Jazz Press	Bart Marantz	Bart Marantz	5 1/2	Latin/Bossa
"Miami Wise"	Concept Music	Bob Meyer	Bob Meyer	4	Latin
"Ornithology"	Hal Leonard	Parker/Harris	Roger Pemberton	5 1/2	Swing
"Perdido"	Kendor Music & Tizol	Lengsfelder/Drake	Matt Harris	3 1/2	Swing
"Quick Silver"	C.L. Barnhouse	Jeff Lowden	Jeff Lowden	5 1/2	Swing
"Sea Breeze"	Neil Kjos	Bobby Shew	Bobby Shew	4	Rock
"Sister Sadie"	Hal Leonard	Horace Silver	Alf Clausen	3 1/2	Shuffle
"Some Skunk Funk"	Kendor Music	Randy Brecker	Jeff Holmes	6	Fusion/Rock
"Things Ain't the Way They Use to Be	Kendor Music	Ellington/Persons	Matt Harris	3	Swing
"Valse Hot"	Hal Leonard	Sonny Rollins	Roger Pemberton	4	Jazz Waltz

Three-Horn Combo Charts

Title	Arranger	Publisher	Series	Grade	Type/Feel
"Angel Eyes"	Harris	Kendor	Jazz Combo	Intermediate	Swing
"Doublethink"	Shutack	Kendor	Doug Beach Music for Combos	Intermediate	Swing
Jazz Combo Pak #10	Mantooth	Hal Leonard	Jazz Combo Paks	Intermediate	Swing
Jazz Combo Pak #18	Mantooth	Hal Leonard	Jazz Combo Paks	Intermediate	Swing
"Kansas City"	Strommen	Kendor	Jazz Combo	Easy	Swing
"Lady Bird"	Mintzer	Kendor	Jazz Combo	Easy	Swing
"The Magic Shop"	Brookmeyer	Kendor	Jazz Combo	Advanced	Swing
"Midnight in Moscow"	Dedrick	Kendor	Jazz Combo	Easy	Swing
"Red-Eye"	DiBlasio	Kendor	Pro Jam Combo	Advanced	Latin
"Samba Solstice"	Schneider	Kendor	Pro Jam Combo	Advanced	Latin
"Some Skunk Funk"	Holmes	Kendor	Jazz Combo	Advanced	Funk

Four-Horn Combo Charts

Title	Arranger	Publisher	Series	Grade	Type/Feel
"Basin Street Blues"	Goodwin	Hal Leonard	Easy Jazz Combo	Easy	Swing
"Bella Bossa"	Thomas	Warner Bros.	Play & Learn	Easy	Latin
"Brazil"	Wolpe	Warner Bros.	Club Date Combo	Intermediate	Latin
"Bye Bye Blackbird"	Wolpe	Warner Bros.	Club Date Combo	Advanced	Swing

Four-Horn Combo Charts

"Cottontail"	Wolpe	Warner Bros.	Club Date Combo	Advanced	Swing
"D Blues"	Thomas	Warner Bros.	Play & Learn	Easy	Swing
"Eager Beaver"	Wolpe	Warner Bros.	Club Date Combo	Advanced	Swing
"Emily"	Wolpe	Warner Bros.	Club Date Combo	Intermediate	Jazz Waltz
"Mambo Bambo"	Thomas	Warner Bros.	Play & Learn	Easy	Latin
"Mr. Lucky"	Wolpe	Warner Bros.	Club Date Combo	Intermediate	Swing
"A Night in Tunisia"	Holmes	Hal Leonard	Easy Jazz Combo	Easy	Latin/Swing
"'Round Midnight"	Wolpe	Warner Bros.	Club Date Combo	Advanced	Ballad
"So Nice"	Holmes	Hal Leonard	Easy Jazz Combo	Easy	Latin
"Stars Fell on Alabama	Wolpe	Warner Bros.	Club Date Combo	Intermediate	Ballad
"Tiger of San Pedro"	Lavender	Jenson	Jazz Combo	Intermediate	Fusion
"Tico Tico"	Wolpe	Warner Bros.	Club Date Combo	Advanced	Latin
"Willow Weep for Me"	Wolpe	Warner Bros.	Club Date Combo	Intermediate	Swing
"Woodchopper's Ball"	Holmes	Hal Leonard	Easy Jazz Combo	Easy	Swing

A Selected List of String Arrangements

Title	Arranger	Publisher	Instruments	Grade	Type/Feel
"All Blues"	Yord Widmoser	Schott	2 violins, viola, cello	IV	Slow blues
"Aquanaut"	Don Palmer	Synthe-Strings	2 violins, viola, cello, rhythm section	V	Latin
"Arcturus"	Julie Lyonn Lieberman	Huiksi Music	2 violins, cello, piano	V	Contemp.
"Baker's Shuffle"	David Baker	Baker	2 violins, viola, cello, bass, rhythm section	V	Swing
"Black-eyed Peas and Corn Bread"	David Baker	Baker	2 violins, viola, cello, bass, rhythm section	IV	Funk
"Blue Strings"	David Baker	Baker	2 violins, viola, cello, bass, rhythm section	IV	Swing
"Blues"	David Baker	Baker	2 violins, viola, cello, bass, rhythm section	IV	Gospel Blues
"Body and Soul"	Calvin Custer	Warner Bros.	2 violins, viola, cello, bass, rhythm section	IV	Ballad
"Bossa Nuovo"	Don Palmer	Synthe-Strings	2 violins, viola, cello, rhythm section	IV	Latin
"Calypso Nova #2"	David Baker	Baker	2 violins, viola, cello, bass, rhythm section	IV	Latin
"Clowning"	Don Palmer	Synthe-Strings	2 violins, viola, cello, rhythm section	V	Rock
"Collage Mirage"	Don Palmer	Synthe-Strings	2 violins, viola, cello, rhythm section	VI	Multi-meter
Darol Anger Originals	Darol Anger	Fiddlistics Music	2 violins, viola, cello	III, IV	Varied
"Dave's Here"	John Radd	MMB Music	2 violins, viola, cello, rhythm section	III	Shuffle Blues
"Eastern Delight"	Don Palmer	Synthe-Strings	2 violins, viola, cello, rhythm section	VII	Multi-meter

A Selected List of String Arrangements

"El Gozo"	Don Palmer	Synthe-Strings	2 violins, viola, cello, rhythm section	V	Bossa nova
"Embraceable You"	Calvin Custer	Warner Bros.	2 violins, viola, cello, rhythm section	IV	Ballad
"Evening Song"	David Baker	Baker	2 violins, viola, cello, bass, rhythm section	IV	Ballad
"Fantasia"	Bert Konowitz	Plan-It, Inc.	2 violins, viola, cello, bass, alto sax	IV	Third Stream
"Fiddlin'"	David Baker	Baker	2 violins, viola, cello, bass, rhythm section	IV	Swing
"Five Pieces for String Quartet"	Miriam Rabson	E & R Music	2 violins, viola, cello	IV–V	Varied
"Glide Stride"	Don Palmer	Synthe-Strings	2 violins, viola, cello, rhythm section	IV	Latin
"Goodbye Porkpie Hat"	August Watters	Watters Music	2 violins, viola, cello	IV	Ballad
"Guess What"	Don Palmer	Synthe Strings	2 violins, viola, cello, rhythm section	VI	Funk
"Holiday for Strings"	Calvin Custer	Warner Bros.	2 violins, viola, cello, rhythm section	V	Latin
"I Remember Clifford	August Watters	Watters Music	2 violins, viola, cello	IV	Ballad
"Jose's Blues"	Randel Sabien	MMB Music	2 violins, viola, cello, rhythm section	IV	Blues
"Joey's Blues"	Jost H. Hecker	Schott Music	2 violins, viola, cello	IV	Blues
"Joshua"	Randel Sabien	MMB Music	2 violins, viola, cello, rhythm section	IV	Contemp.
"Just One of Those Things"	Calvin Custer	Warner Bros.	2 violins, viola, cello,	IV	Swing
"La Crescenta"	Don Palmer	Synthe-Strings	2 violins, viola, cello, rhythm section	V	Latin
"Legacy"	Antonio García	Writer's Block Music	2 violins, viola, cello, piano	V	Varied
"Like Velvet"	Don Palmer	Synthe-Strings	2 violins, viola, cello, rhythm section	II–III	Latin
"Love Is You"	Don Palmer	Synthe-Strings	2 violins, viola, cello, rhythm section	III	Ballad
"Misty"	Calvin Custer	Warner Bros.	2 violins, viola, cello, rhythm section, solo B-flat clarinet	IV	Ballad
Modern Jazz Classics	David Balakrishnan	Fiddlistics Music	2 violins, viola, cello	IV	Varied
"My Funny Valentine"	Calvin Custer	Warner Bros.	2 violins, viola, cello, rhythm section	IV	Ballad
"My One and Only Love"	August Watters	Watters Music	2 violins, viola, cello	IV	Ballad
"Serenity"	Don Palmer	Synthe-Strings	2 violins, viola, cello, rhythm section	V	Ballad
"Slip a Little New"	August Watters	Watters Music	2 violins, viola, cello	V	Ballad

A Selected List of String Arrangements

"Slow Groove"	David Baker	Baker	2 violins, viola, cello, rhythm section	IV	Modal
"Sir Duke"	Steve Wonder	Schott Music	2 violins, viola, cello	IV	Swing
"Sophisticated Lady"	August Watters	Watters Music	2 violins, viola, cello	IV	Ballad
"Street Stuff"	Darol Anger	Fiddlistics Music	2 violins, viola, cello	V & VI	Swing
"String Quartet #1: Ballapadam"	David Balakrishnan	Fiddlistics Music	2 violins, viola, cello	IV-V	Third Stream
"String a Ling"	John Radd	MMB Music	2 violins, viola, cello, rhythm section	III	Blues
"Strings 'N Things"	Don Palmer	Synthe-Strings	2 violins, viola, cello, rhythm section	V	Swing
"Synthe-Ship"	Don Palmer	Synthe-Strings	2 violins, viola, cello, rhythm section	VII	Funk
"That's New"	Yord Widmoser	Schott	2 violins, viola, cello	IV	Swing
"The Count"	Don Palmer	Synthe-Strings	2 violins, ciola, cello, rhythm section	IV	Swing
"The Jamaican Strut"	David Baker	Baker	2 violins, viola, cello, rhythm section	V	Latin
"The First Day of Spring"	David Baker	Baker	2 violins, viola, cello, rhythm section	IV	Waltz
"The Triplet Blues"	David Baker	Baker	2 violins, viola, cello, rhythm section	IV	Blues
TISQ Interprets the Classix: #1, 2	Darol Anger	Fiddlistics Music	2 violins, viola, cello	IV–VI	Varied
"Whisper Not"	August Watters	Watters Music	2 violins, viola, cello	IV	Swing
"Who Do You Think You Are Collection"	Balakrishnan, Anger, Seidenberg	Fiddlistics Music	2 violins, viola, cello	III–VI	Varied

For extensive reviews of arrangements and equipment, see the *Jazz Educators Journal,* September and November 1995, "Watch Out!" column by John Kuzmich, Jr.: "Wire Choir Can Be Electrifying: Parts I & II." For a list of titles, see *Jazz String Ensembles* by Walter J. Straiton, *Jazz Educators Journal,* Dec./Jan. 1984, pp. 21–22, 105.

A Selected List of Vocal Jazz Ensemble Arrangements

Title	Comp./Arranger	Voicing	Style	RS	GR.	Pub.
"Blue Monk"	Cross	SATB	Swing	Y	1	UNC
"Bourée"	Swingle	SATB	Chamber	N	1	WS
"Blues down to My Shoes"	Shaw	2/3 pt	Swing	Y	1	UNC
"I Don't Know Why"	Ames	SSAB	Ballad	N	1	UNC
"Let's Fly"	Schwartz	2 pt	Waltz	Y	1	UNC
"Moonglow"	Hudson/Chinn	SATB	Swing	Y	1	SPR
"Muffin Man"	Cross	SATB	Swing	Y	1	UNC
"Swing Time"	Shaw	SATB	Swing	Y	1	HL
"Tuxedo Junction"	Nowak	SATB	Swing	Y	1	HL

A Selected List of Vocal Jazz Ensemble Arrangements

"I'll Be Seeing You"	Kahn-Fain/Mattson	SATB	Swing	N	2	HL
"I've Got You under My Skin"	Porter/Mattson	SATB	Swing	Y	2	HL
"Peace"	Silver/Weir	SATB	Ballad	Y	2	UNC
"Route 66"	Averre	SATB/SAB	Swing	Y	2	HL
"Satin Doll"	Ellington/Shaw	SATB	Swing	Y	2	HL
"Scat Blues in C"	Crenshaw	SATB	Swing	Y	2	UNC
"Smile"	Zegree	SATB	Ballad	N	2	HL
"Someone to Watch over Me"	Gershwin/Cherin	SATB	Ballad	N	2	Jen/ HL
"The Boy from New York City"	Shaw	SATB	Swing	Y	2	WB
"The Shadow of Your Smile"	Mandel/Puerling	SATB	Ballad	Y	2	Col
"There Is Only You"	Mazur	SATB	Swing	Y	2	UNC
"When I Fall in Love"	Shaw	SATB	Ballad	N	2	HL
"'s Wonderful"	Mattson	SATB	Swing	Y	3	HL
"All Blues"	Davis/Ames	SATB/SSAB	Swing	Y	3	UNC
"A Sleeping Bee"	Weir	SATB	Swing	Y	3	UNC
"Alright, OK, You Win"	Zegree	SATB	Swing	Y	3	HL
"Angel Eyes"	Denis/Weir	SATB	Lat./Swg.	Y	3	Aber
"Desafinado"	Mattson	SATB	Latin	Y	3	Ken
"Embraceable You"	Mattson	SATB	Ballad	N	3	PM
"Fly Me to the Moon"	Howard/Shaw	SATB	Swing	Y	3	UNC
"Full Moon"	Broadley	SATB	Latin	Y	3	UNC
"Georgia on My Mind"	Carmichael/Puerling	SATB	Ballad	Y	3	Col
"Georgia on My Mind"	Carmichael/Puerling	SATB	Swing	Y	3	HL
"I've Got the World on a String"	Weir	SATB	Swing	Y	3	UNC
"Is You Is or Is You Ain't My Baby"	Rutherford	SATB	Swing	Y	3	HL
"Joy"	Niewood/Buffa	SATB	Latin	Y	3	UNC
"More I Cannot Wish You"	Mattson	SATB	Ballad	N	3	HL
"More than You Know"	Zegree	SATB	Ballad	N	3	HL
"Moving Up"	Broadley	SATB	Funk	Y	3	UNC
"Mr. Flat Five"	Broadley	SATB	Swing	Y	3	UNC
"Red Clay"	Hubbard/Buffa	SATB	Funk	Y	3	UNC
"'Round Midnight"	Monk/Buffa	SATB	Ballad	Y	3	UNC
"Seems like Old Times"	Puerling	SATB	Swing	Y	3	HL

A Selected List of Vocal Jazz Ensemble Arrangements

"South of the Border"	Broadley	SATB	Latin	Y	3	UNC
"Spain"	Corea/Crenshaw	SATB	Latin	Y	3	UNC
"Take the A Train"	Ellington/Zegree	SATB	Swing	Y	3	HL
"That Cat Is High"	MT/Mazur	SATB	Doo Wop	Y	3	UNC
"Up Jumped Spring"	Hubbard/Cross	SATB	Swing	Y	3	UNC
"Africa"	Paich/Porcaro/ Crenshaw	SATB	Contemp.	N	4	UNC
"Alice in Wonderland"	Treece	SSATBB	Ballad	N	4	UNC
"All the Things You Are"	Swingle	SATB	Ballad	N	4	UNC
"Come Rain or Come Shine"	Puerling	SATB	Swing	Y	4	HL
"Dare the Moon"	Meader	SSATB	Swing	Y	4	UNC
"Four Brothers"	Giuffre/Mazur	SATB	Swing	Y	4	UNC
"How Long Has This Been Going On?"	Mattson	SATB	Ballad	Y	4	Jen
"I Wish You Love"	Marois	SATB	Ballad	Y	4	UNC
"Nightingale Sang in Berkeley Square"	Puerling	SATB	Ballad	N	4	HL
"Singin' in the Rain"	Arabian-Tini	SSATBB	Swing	N	4	UNC
"The Christmas Song"	Tormé/Puerling	SATB	Ballad	Y	4	HL

RS=Rhythm Section, G=Grade 1-5, easiest to most challenging, Pub=Publisher
Aber=Aberdeen Col=Columbia HL=Hal Leonard Jen=Jenson Ken=Kendor PM=Phil Mattson
SPR=Studio PR UNC=UNC Jazz Press WB=Warner Brothers

List of Selected Publishers and Retailers

Advanced Music
P.O. Box 11117
Marina Del Ray, CA 90295

Advance Music
Maierackerstr. 18
7407 Rottenburg N.
Germany

Alfred Publishing
16380 Roscoe Boulevard
P.O. Box 10003
Van Nuys, CA 91410-0003

Bob Eberhart Music
P.O. Box 1111
East Lansing, MI 48823

Chas Colin Publishers
315 West 53rd Street
New York, NY 10019

C. L. Barnhouse Publishing
P.O. Box 680
Oskaloosa, IA 52577

Concept Music-Bobby Meyer
6705 N. Lamar #251
Austin, TX 78752

CPP Belwin, Inc.
15800 NW 48th Street
Miami, FL 33014

Dallas Jazz Productions
4305 Pine Ridge Drive
Garland, TX 75042

David Baker
1940 Marilyn Drive
Bloomington, IN 47401

David Metzger Music
547 Greencrest Street N.E.
Salem, OR 97301

DCI Music Video
541 Avenue of the Americas
New York, NY 10011

Descarga
328 Flatbush Avenue, Ste. 180
Brooklyn, NY 11238

Doug Beach Music
c/o Kendor Music

DPZ Music
P.O. Box 59659
Dallas, TX 75229

DVS Music-Don Schamber
3 Forrest Knoll Road
Monterey, CA 93940

Education Software
934 Forest Avenue
Oak Park, IL 60302

Ellis Music Enterprises
c/o Mr. Curtis Bradshaw
Eastfield College
3737 Motley Drive
Mesquite, TX 75150

E & R Music Printers
67 King Street
Oberlin, OH 4407

Fiddlistics Music
P.O. Box 19297
Oakland, CA 94619

Hal Leonard Publishing
7777 West Bluemound Road
P.O. Box 13819
Milwaukee, WI 52313

Hansen House
1820 West Avenue
Miami Beach, FL 33139

Houston Publishing
224 S. Lebanon Street
Lebanon, IN 46052

Huiksi Music
P.O. Box 495
New York, NY 10024

Jamey Aebersold-Jazz Aids
P.O. Box 1244
New Albany, IN 47150

Jobar Music-Mike Barone
P.O. Box 349
New Castle, CO 81647

J. W. Pepper
P.O. Box 850
Valley Forge, PA 19482

Kendor Music
P.O. Box 278
Delevan, NY 14042

King Brand Co.
Classic Editions
250 W 49th Street, Suite 404
New York, NY 10019

Machu Picchu Prod.-Ladd McIntosh
7712 Alcove Avenue
N. Hollywood, CA 91605

Margun Music, Inc.
167 Dudley Road
Newton Centre, MA 02159

Marina Music Service
P.O. Box 46159
Seattle, WA 98126

Mel Bay Music
#4 Industrial Drive
Pacific, MO 63069

Melody Maker Press
300 Oak Street
Hollywood, FL 33019

MiBac Music Software
Box 468
Northfield, MN 55047

MMB Music
The Contemporary Arts Building
3526 Washington Avenue
St. Louis, MO 63103

Modern String Quartet
c/o Schott Music International
Weihergarten 5
D-55116 Mainz
Germany

Music Exchange
151 W 46th Street
New York, NY 10036

Onondaga Music Service
412 S. Clinton Street
Syracuse, NY 13202

Paul Lohorn
P.O. Box 80095
Chattanooga, TN 37411

P & D Publications
4453 Wesley Way
Austell, GA 30001

Pender's Music
314 S. Elm Street
Denton, TX 76201

Plan-It Inc.
Box 378
Syosset, NY 11791

Prentice Hall, Inc.
Route 9W
Inglewood Cliffs, NJ 07632

Roger Myers
P.O. Box 56669
Riverside, CA 92517

Sam Fox Publishing
170 NE 33rd Street
Miami, FL 33307

Second Floor Music
130 West 28th Street, 2nd Fl.
New York, NY, 10001-6108

Shawnee Press
Delaware Water Gap, PA 18327

Sher Music
P.O. Box 445
Petaluma, CA 94953

Sierra Music
P.O. Box 543
Liberty Lake, WA 99019

S. O. S. Music Services
1817 29th Avenue E
Tuscaloosa, AL 35405

Sound Music Publications
P.O. Box 598
Lynnwood, WA 98046-0598

Speigl Music
2816 Shady Glen
Orange, CA 92667

Stanton Music
30030 S. 4th Street
Columbus, OH 43215

Steve Wright
15631 Lexington Circle
Minnetonka, MN 55343

Summit Music Pub
846 Summit Avenue
St. Paul, MN 55105

Synthe-Strings
3048 Cloudcrest
La Crescenta, CA 91214

Temporal Acuity Products
300 120th Avenue NE, Bldg. 1
Bellevue, WA 98005

UNC Jazz Press
Jazz Studies
University of Northern Colorado
Greeley, CO 80639

Union Dues-Neal Finn
250 Sund Avenue
Ben Lamond, CA 95005

Walrus Music Publishing
P.O. Box 11267
Glendale, CA 91226-7267

Warner Brothers
265 Secaucus Road
Secaucus, NJ 07096-2037

August Watters Music Publishing
P.O. Box 180242
Boston, MA 02111

William Allen Music
P.O. Box 790
Newington, VA 22122

William C. Brown Company
2460 Kerper Boulevard
Dubuque, IA 52001

Writer's Block Music Publications
c/o Antonio J. García
8052 Keeler Avenue
Skokie, IL 60076-3232

A Selected List of Jazz Artists

Jazz Composers

Ornette Coleman
John Coltrane
Chick Corea
Tadd Dameron
Miles Davis
Duke Ellington
Dizzy Gillespie
Benny Golson
Herbie Hancock
Charles Mingus
Thelonious Monk
Charlie Parker
Sonny Rollins
Wayne Shorter
Horace Silver
Billy Strayhorn
Joe Zawinul

Standard-Tune Composers

Harold Arlen
Sammy Cahn and
Jimmy Van Heusen
Hoagy Carmichael
Matt Dennis
George Gershwin
Jerome Kern
Lerner and Lowe
Cole Porter
Richard Rodgers
Fats Waller
Kurt Weill
Victor Young

Arrangers

Toshiko Akiyoshi
Bob Brookmeyer
Gil Evans
Frank Foster
Gil Fuller
Bill Holman
Quincy Jones
Thad Jones
Billy May
Bob Mintzer
Sammy Nestico
Lennie Niehaus
Chico O'Farrill
Johnny Richards
George Russell
Maria Schneider
Gerald Wilson

Vocalists

Louis Armstrong
Tony Bennett

Betty Carter
Nat King Cole
Billy Eckstein
Ella Fitzgerald
Jon Hendricks
Billie Holiday
Shirley Horn
Eddie Jefferson
Sheila Jordan
Cleo Laine
Bobby McFerrin
Mark Murphy
Anita O'Day
Dianne Reeves
Diane Schuur
Frank Sinatra
Bessie Smith
Mel Tormé
Sarah Vaughan
Dinah Washington
Joe Williams
Cassandra Wilson
Nancy Wilson

Vocal Groups

Beachfront Property
Double Six
Four Freshmen
The Hi-Los
Lambert, Hendricks, and Ross
Manhattan Transfer
The New York Voices
The Nylons
Phil Mattson and the P. M. Singers
Rare Silk
The Real Group
The Ritz
Swingle Singers
Singers Unlimited
Take 6
2 + 2

Vocal Arrangers

April Arabian-Tini
Todd Buffa
David Cazier
Clare Fischer
Gary Fry
Phil Mattson
Darmon Meader
Susan Moniger
Gene Puerling
Paris Rutherford
Kirby Shaw
Ward Swingle
Roger Treece
Michele Weir
Steve Zegree

String Groups

Black Swan
Boccerini Ensemble
David Grisman Quintet
Hot Club of France
Leroy Jenkins (and Strings)
Really Eclectic String Quartet
Soldier String Quartet
Straight Ahead
String Trio of New York
Turtle Island String Quartet
Uptown String Quartet

Big Band Leaders

Toshiko Akiyoshi and Lew Tabackin
Count Basie
Tommy Dorsey
Billy Eckstine
Duke Ellington
Maynard Ferguson
Benny Goodman
Fletcher Henderson
Woody Herman
Earl Hines
Thad Jones and Mel Lewis
Stan Kenton
Jimmie Lunceford
Machito
Rob McConnell
Glenn Miller
Bob Mintzer
Tito Puente
Sun Ra
Buddy Rich
Eddie Sauter and Bill Finegan
Chick Webb

Latin Jazz Artists

Ray Barretto
Mario Bauza
Celia Cruz
Astrud Gilberto
João Gilberto
Jerry Gonzalez
Giovanni Hidalgo
Machito
Eddie Palmieri
Tito Puente
Tito Rodriguez
Gonzalo Rubalcaba
Hilton Ruiz
Poncho Sanchez

Trumpet

Louis Armstrong
Chet Baker
Guido Basso
Bix Beiderbecke
Randy Brecker
Clifford Brown
Don Cherry
Miles Davis
Harry "Sweets" Edison
Roy Eldridge
Maynard Ferguson
Dizzy Gillespie
Freddie Hubbard
Thad Jones
Wynton Marsalis
Lee Morgan
Fats Navarro
Red Rodney
Woody Shaw
Clark Terry
Cootie Williams

Trombone

Ray Anderson
Carl Fontana
Curtis Fuller
Urbie Green
Slide Hampton

Conrad Herwig
J. J. Johnson
Albert Mangelsdorff
Ian McDougall
Joe "Tricky" Sam Nanton
Kid Ory
Frank Rosolino
Jack Teagarden
Steve Turre
Bill Watrous
Dicky Wells
Kai Winding

Valve Trombone/ Euphonium

Ashley Alexander
Bob Brookmeyer
Rich Matteson
Rob McConnell

Tuba

Bill Barber
Howard Johnson
Rich Matteson

Flute

Eric Dolphy
Joe Farrell
Paul Horn (Canada)
Raashan Roland Kirk
Hubert Laws
James Moody
Bud Shank
Lew Tabackin
Frank Wess

Clarinet

Barney Bigard
Don Byron
Eddie Daniels
Buddy DeFranco
Johnny Dodds
Benny Goodman
Jimmy Hamilton
Phil Nominees
Artie Shaw

Strings

Darol Anger, violin
David Balakrishnan, violin
David Baker, cello
John Blake, violin
Johnny Frigo, violin
Matt Glaser, violin
Stéphane Grappelli, violin
Sugar Cane Harris, violin
Fred Katz, cello
Joe Kennedy Jr., violin
Harry Lookofsky, violin
Mark O'Connor, violin
Jean-Luc Ponty, violin
Maxine Roach, viola
Randy Sabien, violin
Stuff Smith, violin
Eddie South, violin
Michael Urbaniak, violin
Joe Venuti, violin
Claude Williams, violin

Piano

Count Basie
Nat King Cole
Chick Corea
Bill Evans
Tommy Flanagan
Erroll Garner
Herbie Hancock
Barry Harris
Earl Hines
Keith Jarrett
James P. Johnson
Wynton Kelly
Marian McPartland
Thelonious Monk
Oscar Peterson
Bud Powell
George Shearing
Cecil Taylor
Art Tatum
McCoy Tyner
Fats Waller
Mary Lou Williams
Teddy Wilson

Organ

Charles Earland
Richard "Groove" Holmes
Jack McDuff
Jimmy Smith
Larry Young

Guitar

John Abercrombie
George Benson
Kenny Burrell
Charlie Christian
Herb Ellis
Freddie Green
Grant Green
Tal Farlow
Jim Hall
Barney Kessel
Pat Martino
John McLaughlin
Wes Montgomery
Pat Metheny
Joe Pass
Jimmy Raney
Django Reinhardt
John Scofield

Bass

Jimmy Blanton
Ray Brown
Ron Carter
Paul Chambers
Stanley Clarke
Eddie Gomez
Charlie Haden
Milt Hinton
Dave Holland
Scott LaFaro
Charles Mingus
Walter Page
Jaco Pastorius
Niels-Henning Orsted Pedersen
Oscar Pettiford
Rufus Reid

Drums/Percussion

Louie Bellson
Ed Blackwell
Art Blakey
Kenny Clarke
Billy Cobham
Jack DeJohnette
Peter Erskine

Steve Gadd
Roy Haynes
Billy Higgins
Elvin Jones
Jo Jones
Philly Joe Jones
Mel Lewis
Airto Moriera
Paul Motian
Tito Puente
Buddy Rich
Max Roach
Ed Thigpen
Tony Williams

Vibraphone

Gary Burton
Lionel Hampton
Bobby Hutcherson
Milt Jackson
Mike Manieri
Red Norvo

Saxophone

Soprano

Sidney Bechet
Jane Ira Bloom
Anthony Braxton
John Coltrane
Jan Garbarek
Steve Lacey
David Liebman
Wayne Shorter

Alto

Cannonball Adderley
Benny Carter
Ornette Coleman
Paul Desmond
Eric Dolphy
Johnny Hodges
Moe Koffman
Lee Konitz
Jackie McLean
Charlie Parker
Art Pepper
Marshall Royal
Sonny Stitt
Phil Woods

Tenor

Gene Ammons
Michael Brecker
John Coltrane
Stan Getz
Dexter Gordon
Coleman Hawkins
Jimmy Heath
Joe Henderson
Branford Marsalis
Sonny Rollins
Pharoah Sanders
Wayne Shorter
Zoot Sims
Ben Webster
Lester Young

Baritone

Pepper Adams
Nick Brignola
Harry Carney
Serge Chaloff
Ronnie Cuber
Gerry Mulligan
John Surman

A Selected Jazz Listening List

Artist	Instrument	Title	Recording Number
Adderley, Cannonball	Alto Saxophone	*At the Lighthouse* with Nat Adderley, Sam Jones, V. Feldman, L. Hayes	Landmark 1305
Adderley, Cannonball	Alto Saxophone	*Something Else* with Miles Davis	BST 81595
Adderley, Cannonball	Alto Saxophone	*Takes Charge* with Wynton Kelly, Paul Chambers, J. Cobb	Landmark 1306
Andrade, Leny	Vocals/Brazilian	*Embraceable You*	Timeless 365, Descarga # TL-11639
Armstrong, Louis	Vocals/Trumpet	*The Hot Fives and Hot Sevens,* Vol. III	Columbia CK 44422
Armstrong, Louis	Vocals/Trumpet	*Louis Armstrong Greatest Hits*	Curb Records D2-77339
Baker, Chet	Trumpet	*The Touch of Your Lips* with Doug Raney, N.H.O. Pederson	Steeplechase 1122
Basie, Count	Jazz Ensemble	*The Best of the Count Basie Big Band*	Pablo 2405-422
Basie, Count with Lambert, Hendricks, & Ross Jazz Ensemble	Vocal Jazz Ensemble	*Sing Along with Basie*	Roulette CDP 7953322
Batacumbele	Afro-Cuban Ensemble	*Afro-Caribbean Jazz*	Montuno 525, Descarga # TL-10190
Bauza, Mario	Afro-Cuban Ensemble	*Afro-Cuban Jazz*	Caiman 9017, Descarga # TL-01350
Bennett, Tony	Vocals	*Tony Bennett/Bill Evans*	Fantasy F-9489
Blakey, Art	Drums	*Jazz Messengers* with D. Byrd, H. Mobley, H. Silver, D. Watkin	Columbia PC 37021
Blakey, Art	Drums	*Night at Birdland* with C. Brown, Lou Donaldson, H. Silver, C. Russell	Blue Note 81522
Brown, Clifford	Trumpet	*Brown & Roach Inc.* with Sonny Rollins, Max Roach	EmArcy 1010
Brown, Clifford	Trumpet	*Brownie Eyes*	Blue Note LA267-G
Brown, Clifford	Trumpet	*Clifford Brown with Strings*	EmArcy 1011
Brown, Clifford	Trumpet	*Study in Brown* with Harold Land, Max Roach	EmArcy 1008

Artist	Instrument	Title	Recording Number
Brown, Ray	Bass	*Bam, Bam, Bam* with Gene Harris, Jeff Hamilton	Concord 375
Brown, Ray	Bass	*Don't Forget the Blues* with Al Grey, Gene Harris, Grady Tate, Ron Eschete	Concord 293
Carter, Betty	Vocals	*It's Not about the Melody*	Verve 314-513870-2
Cole, Nat King	Vocals	*Love Is Here to Stay*	Capitol SWAK 11355
Coleman, Ornette	Alto Saxophone	*Something Else!* with Don Cherry, Walter Norris	OJC 163
Coleman, Ornette	Alto Saxophone	*This Is Our Music* with Cherry, Haden, Blackwell	Atl. 1353
Coleman, Ornette	Alto Saxophone	*Town Hall Concert* with Izenzohn, Moffett, and strings	ESP 1006
Coltrane, John	Tenor Saxophone	*A Love Supreme* with M. Tyner, J. Garrison, Elvin Jones	MCA 29017
Coltrane, John	Tenor Saxophone	*Blue Train* with C. Fuller, Lee Morgan, Philly Joe Jones	Blue Note 81577
Coltrane, John	Tenor Saxophone	*Crescent* with M. Tyner, J. Garrison, Elvin Jones	MCA 5889
Coltrane, John	Tenor Saxophone	*Giant Steps* with Tommy Flanagan, P. Chambers, A. Taylor	Atlantic 1311
Coltrane, John	Tenor Saxophone	*Impressions* with M. Tyner, J. Garrison, Elvin Jones	MCA 5887
Coltrane, John	Tenor Saxophone	*Live at Birdland* with M. Tyner, J. Garrison, Elvin Jones	MCA 29015
Coltrane, John	Tenor Saxophone	*More Lasting Than Bronze*	Prestige 24014
Corea, Chick	Piano	*Light as aFeather* with Joe Farrell, Stan Clarke, Airto	Polydor 5525
Corea, Chick	Piano	*Now He Sings, Now He Sobs* with Roy Haynes, M. Vitous	BI 90055
Cruz, Celia	Vocals/Afro-Cuban	*The Best of Celia Cruz*	Globo/Sony 080587, Descarga # TL-09212
Davis, Miles	Trumpet	*Jazz at the Plaza* with with J. Coltrane, C. Adderley, Bill Evans	Columbia 32470
Davis, Miles	Trumpet	*Kind of Blue* with J. Coltrane, C. Adderley, W. Kelly, Paul Chambers	Columbia 40579

Artist	Instrument	Title	Recording Number
Davis, Miles	Trumpet	*Miles Davis* (2-record set from 1956-57)	Prestige 24001
Davis, Miles	Trumpet	*Milestones* with J. Coltrane, C. Adderley, Paul Chambers	Columbia 40837
Davis, Miles	Trumpet	*My Funny Valentine* with G. Coleman, R. Carter, H. Hancock	Columbia 9106
Davis, Miles	Trumpet	*Nefertiti* with W. Shorter, R. Carter, T. Williams, H. Hancock	Columbia CS9594
Davis, Miles	Trumpet	*Seven Steps to Heaven* with H. Hancock, R. Carter, T. Williams	Columbia CS8851
Davis, Miles	Trumpet/Nonet	*Birth of the Cool*	Capitol CDP 792862
DeFranco, Buddy	Clarinet	*The Complete Verve Buddy DeFranco / Sonny Clark*	Mosaic MR 117
Ellington, Duke	Jazz Ensemble	*Blanton, Webster Band*	VJC-1003-2
Ellington, Duke	Jazz Ensemble	*At Newport*	Columbia 40587
Ellington, Duke	Jazz Ensemble	*Black, Brown, and Beige*	RCA Bluebird 86641
Evans, Bill	Piano	*Sunday at the Village Vanguard*	Original Jazz Classics OJC 140
Evans, Bill	Piano	*The Solo Sessions,* Vol.1	Milestone M 9170
Fischer, Clare & 2 + 2	Vocal Jazz Ensemble/ Brazilian	*Salsa Picante*	Discovery DS-817
Fitzgerald, Ella	Vocals	*Cole Porter Songbook*	Verve VE-2-2511
Fitzgerald, Ella	Vocals	*Duke Ellington Songbook*	Verve 837 035, 6, 7, & 8 -2
Gil Evans Orchestra	Jazz Ensemble	*Out of the Cool*	MCACD 9653
Gilberto, João	Instr. & Vocal/ Brazilian	*Stan Getz & Astrud...*	Verve/Polygram 810048, Descarga # TL-12633
Gillespie, Dizzy	Afro-Cuban Ensemble	*Afro-Cuban Jazz Moods with Machito*	Pablo/Fantasy OJC447, Descarga # TL-01348
Gillespie, Dizzy	Bebop	*Shaw 'Nuff*	Musicraft MVSCD-53
Gonzalez, Jerry	Afro-Cuban Ensemble	*Rumba Para Monk*	Sunnyside SSC1036D, Descarga # TL-10502
Grappelli, Stéphane	Violin	*Tivoli Gardens, Copenhagen, Denmark*	Original Jazz Classics OJC 441

Artist	Instrument	Title	Recording Number
Hancock, Herbie	Piano	*Empyrean Isles* with F. Hubbard, R. Carter, T. Williams	Blue Note 84175
Hancock, Herbie	Piano	*Maiden Voyage* with F. Hubbard, R. Carter, T. Williams	Blue Note 84195
Hancock, Herbie	Piano	*The Best of Herbie Hancock*	BI 91142
Hancock, Herbie	Piano	*The Prisoner* with Joe Henderson, Johnny Coles	Blue Note 84321
Henderson, Joe	Tenor Saxophone	*Inner Urge* with Elvin Jones, M. Tyner, B. Cranshaw	Blue Note 84189
Henderson, Joe	Tenor Saxophone	*Live in Japan*	Milestone 9047
Henderson, Joe	Tenor Saxophone	*Power to the People* with H. Hancock, R. Carter, J. DeJohnette	Milestone 9024
Hendricks, Jon	Vocals	*Cloudburst*	enja EJA-CD-4032
Hi-Los	Vocal Jazz Ensemble	*Harmony in Jazz*	P Encore 1438
Holiday, Billie	Vocals	*God Bless the Child*	Columbia G 30782
Horn, Shirley	Vocals	*Here's to Life*	Verve 314-511879-2
Hubbard, Freddie	Trumpet	*Hub of Hubbard* with E. Daniels, R. Hanna	MPS 15 267
Hubbard, Freddie	Trumpet	*Keep Your Soul Together*	CTI 6036
Hubbard, Freddie	Trumpet	*Ready for Freddie* with W. Shorter, Elvin Jones, M. Tyner	Blue Note 84085
Hubbard, Freddie	Trumpet	*Sky Dive*	CTI 6018
Jackson, Milt	Vibes	*Bags Meets Wes!* with Wes Montgomery, W. Kelly, S. Jones, Philly Joe Jones	OJC 234
Jefferson, Eddie	Vocals	*Things Are Getting Better*	Muse MR 5043
Johnson, J. J.	Trombone	*The Eminent J. J. Vol. 1 & 2* with C. Brown, H. Mobley	Blue Note 81505 & 81506
Johnson, J. J.	Trombone	*The Trombone Master* with T. Flanagan, P. Chambers, M. Roach	Columbia CJ44443
Jones, Elvin	Drums	*Live at the Lighthouse* with Liebman & Grossman	Blue Note LA015-G2
Jones, Elvin	Drums	*Live at Village Vanguard*	enja 2036
Lambert, Hendricks, & Ross	Vocal Jazz Ensemble	*Greatest Hits*	Columbia C 32911

Artist	Instrument	Title	Recording Number
Lambert, Hendricks, &Ross	Vocal Jazz Ensemble	*Sing a Song of Basie*	Impulse GRD-112
Lincoln, Abbey	Vocals	*Talking to the Sun*	enja ENJ-CD-4060
Lopez, "Cachao"	Afro-Cuban Ensemble	*Master Sessions,* Vol. 1	Crescent Moon/Epic 64320, Descarga # TL-13328
Machito	Afro-Cuban Ensemble	*Machito & His Afro-Cubans*	Fania 73, Descarga # TL-06530
Manhattan Transfer	Vocal Jazz Ensemble	*Vocalese*	Atlantic 81266-1
Marsalis, Wynton	Trumpet	*Standard Time* with M. Roberts, Bob Hurst, Jeff Watts	Columbia FC 40461
McFerrin, Bobby	Vocals	*Play* with Chick Corea	Blue Note B21Z-95477
McPartland, Marian	Piano	*Plays the Benny Carter Songbook*	Concord CCD 4412
McRae, Carmen	Vocals	*Carmen Sings Monk*	Novus 3086-2-N
Mitchell, Roscoe	Alto Saxophone	*Congliptious*	Nessa - 2
Modern Jazz Quartet	Piano, Bass, Drums, Vibraphone	*MJQ40*	Atlantic 7 82330 2
Monk, Thelonious	Piano	*Monk & Trane*	Milestone 47011
Montgomery, Wes	Guitar	*Full House* with Johnny Griffin, W. Kelly, P. Chambers	OJC 106
Montgomery, Wes	Guitar	*The Small Group Recordings*—Live with W. Kelly, P. Chambers	Verve 833-555-1
Montgomery, Wes	Guitar	*Trio* with Melvin Rhyne, Paul Parker	OJC 034
Morgan, Lee	Trumpet	*Cornbread* with H. Hancock, J. McLean, H. Mobley	Blue Note 84222
Murphy, Mark	Vocals	*The Artistry of...*	Muse MR 5286
Nelson, Oliver	Tenor Saxophone	*Blues & the Abstract Truth*	MCA 5659
New York Voices	Vocal Jazz Ensemble	*New York Voices*	GRP GRD-9589
Palmieri, Eddie	Afro-Cuban Ensemble	*The Best of...*	Tico 1317, Descarga # TL-09218
Parker, Charlie	Alto Saxophone	*Jazz at Massey Hall* with M. Roach, B. Powell, Dizzy Gillespie	Prestige 24024
Parker, Charlie	Alto Saxophone	*Now's the Time*	Verve 8005
Parker, Charlie	Alto Saxophone	*The Savoy Recordings*	Savoy 2201

Artist	Instrument	Title	Recording Number
Parker, Charlie	Alto Saxophone	*The Verve Years—Four Small Groups*	Verve 827-154-1
Powell, Bud	Piano	*The Amazing Bud Powell,* Vol. 1	Blue Note 781503
Puente, Tito	Afro-Cuban Ensemble	*The Mambo King 100th LP*	Sony 80680CD, Descarga # TL-09246
Reeves, Dianne	Vocals	*I Remember*	Blue Note B21S-90264
Rodriguez, Tito	Afro-Cuban Ensemble	*Big Band Latino*	Palladium PCD5117, Descarga # TL-10442
Rollins, Sonny	Tenor Saxophone	*Newk's Time* with W. Kelly, D. Watkins, Philly Joe Jones	Blue Note 84001
Rollins, Sonny	Tenor Saxophone	*Now's the Time* with Ron Carter, Herbie Hancock	QJ 25241
Rollins, Sonny	Tenor Saxophone	*Saxophone Collosos & More* with C. Brown, M. Roach	Prestige 24050
Rollins, Sonny	Tenor Saxophone	*Sonny Rollins with John Coltrane*	Prestige 24004
Rollins, Sonny	Tenor Saxophone	*The Bridge* with Jim Hall, B. Cranshaw	RCA2527
Rubalcaba, Gonzalo	Afro-Cuban Ensemble	*Live in Havana*	Messidor 15960, Descarga # TL-10244
Ruiz, Hilton	Afro-Cuban Ensemble	*A Moment's Notice*	BMG 3123-2-N, Descarga # TL-10602
Sanchez, Poncho	Afro-Cuban Ensemble	*Papa Gato*	Picante/Concord 4310 Descarga # TL-07524
Shorter, Wayne	Tenor Saxophone	*Speak No Evil* with Freddie Hubbard, H. Hancock, E. Jones	Blue Note 84194
Silver, Horace	Piano	*Blowin' the Blues Away* with B. Mitchell, Jr. Cook	Blue Note 84017
Silver, Horace	Piano	*Song for My Father* with Carmel Jones, Joe Henderson	Blue Note 84185
Silver, Horace	Piano	*The Cape Verdean Blues* with J. J. Johnson, W. Shaw, J. Henderson	Blue Note 84220
Singers Unlimited	Vocal Jazz Ensemble	*Just in Time*	Pausa PR 7048
Stitt, Sonny	Alto Saxophone	*The Stitt/Rollins Session* with Dizzy Gillespie	Verve 833-588-1
Stitt, Sonny	Alto/Tenor Saxophone	*Constellation* with Barry Harris, Sam Jones, Ray Brooks	Muse 5323
Thad Jones/ Mel Lewis Orchestra	Jazz Ensemble	*Thad Jones/Mel Lewis*	LRC CDC 9004

Artist	Instrument	Title	Recording Number
Tormé, Mel	Vocals	*Mel & George "Do" World War II* with George Shearing	Concord Jazz CCD-4471
Toshiko Akiyoshi–Lew Tabackin Big Band	Jazz Ensemble	*The Toshiko Akiyoshi—Lew Tabackin Big Band*	Novus ND 83 106
Turtle Island String Quartet	Jazz Strings	*The TISQ*	Windham Hill Jazz 0110
Tyner, McCoy	Piano	*Enlightenment*	Milestone 55001
Tyner, McCoy	Piano	*Reevaluation: The Impulse Years*	MCA 204156
Tyner, McCoy	Piano	*The Early Trios*	MCA 204157
Tyner, McCoy	Piano	*The Real McCoy* with Joe Henderson, R. Carter, E. Jones	Blue Note 84264
Uptown String Quartet	Jazz Strings	*Just Wait a Minute!*	Mesa/Blue Moon R479174
Various Artists	Afro-Cuban Ensemble	*Cuban Big Band Sounds*	Palladium 160, Descarga # TL-10402
Various Artists	Afro-Cuban Ensemble	*The Mambo Kings*	Electra E2 61240, Descarga # TL-10990
Vaughan, Sarah	Vocals	*Live in Japan*	Mainstream 2-J2K-57123
Williams, Joe	Vocals	*Here's to Life*	Telarc Jazz CD-83357
Wilson, Cassandra	Vocals	*Blue Skies*	JMT 834 419-2
Wilson, Nancy	Vocals	*For Once in My Life*	Capitol SF-728
Woods, Phil	Alto Saxophone	*Bouquet* with Tom Harrell, Hal Galper, S. Gilmore, B. Goodwin	Concord 377
Woody Herman Orchestra	Jazz Ensemble	*The Thundering Herds 1945-1947*	CBS 460825
Young, Larry	Organ	*Unity* with Woody Shaw, E. Jones, Joe Henderson	Blue Note 84221

A Selected List of Jazz Improvisation Play-Along Materials

Students and teachers are faced with a tremendous amount of published jazz play-along materials where the listener plays the melody or improvises or both with the accompanying recording of a rhythm section consisting of piano, bass, and drums. The play-alongs fall into two main categories: (1) jazz improvisation methods and (2) tunes. The method category consists primarily of exercises in various keys and progressions for the student. Some, like Willie Thomas's *Jazz Anyone?,* are focused on imitation and call and response. The tune category consists of recordings with compositions (usually jazz standards) that may be used by intermediate through more advanced players.

One of the most widely used series of play-along records is *A New Approach to Jazz Improvisation* by Jamey Aebersold, which now includes more than sixty volumes on CD. The first volume, *A New Approach to Jazz Improvisation,* first appeared in 1967. This series offers well-recorded backgrounds to chord progressions and published "standards" played by some of the finest jazz rhythm-section musicians. Each record also includes accompanying booklets providing transposed melodies and chords for different instruments. Some contain exercises for the beginning improviser.

The volumes for beginning improvisers include:

Volume 1, *A New Approach to Jazz Improvisation*

Volume 24, *Major and Minor*

Volume 21, *Gettin' It Together*

Volume 3, *i–V7–I Progression*

Volume 54, *Maiden Voyage*

Some of these volumes contain a significant amount of printed material for the beginning improviser. The beginner will become familiar with chord and scale relationships and be offered practice examples, patterns, and suggestions.

In Volume 1, the booklet explains that the basic ingredients in jazz improvisation are scales and chords and their relationship. Suggestions for practicing chords, scales, and patterns are introduced at the outset. Aebersold urges students to listen to the album while watching the chord progressions; thus students may make a connection between what they hear on the record and what is notated on the page.

Volume 24, *Major and Minor,* is designed for the beginning improviser. Each track contains only one key center using major or Dorian mode; and the tracks are played in a variety of styles, such as Latin, rock, and swing at various tempos. The best feature of this volume is that each track lasts for three to four minutes, allowing the novice ample time to become acclimated to the key center and possible note choices. Included in this volume is a helpful separate demonstration record, and many suggested melodic ideas are presented. Also, the solo on the demonstration record has been transcribed.

Volume 21, *Gettin' It Together,* is more ambitious for a beginning improviser and introduces advanced concepts and more difficult chord progressions. Aebersold supplies each recorded track with practice suggestions. Modes other than major and Dorian are introduced but perhaps are beyond the capability of the beginning improviser. Included are suggestions for using this volume by band, orchestra, and choir directors. A myriad of melodic patterns is included for the student to use or replace with original ideas.

For those interested in learning how to play Latin jazz, try Volume 64, *Salsa Latin Jazz.* It contains thirteen compositions played in an authentic Latin jazz style. Each volume is rated by level of difficulty from beginning to advanced. These recordings are not methods in the true sense but have filled a void left by the decline of the jam session. They furnish an opportunity for the novice as well as the professional to experiment, express, create, and practice improvisation.

The *Music Minus One* series, in existence for many years, has an extensive catalog of hundreds of volumes running the gamut from chamber music, classical solos, and big band charts to collections of jazz standards. A five-volume jazz improvisation method is available from the catalog as well as Rich Matteson and Jack Peterson's two-volume improvisation method, *The Art of Improvisation.* There are about forty volumes containing play-along compositions for the improviser. The volumes are well-recorded and give the student a chance to perform many jazz standards and some "obscure" compositions. Some volumes are dedicated to different styles or the works of a specific composer. One problem that might appear is that sections of each cut may contain one of the studio musicians improvising for four to eight measures. This provides an example for the user, but may be confusing because the volumes lack accompanying booklets with the recording. However, lead sheets are provided.

LaPorta's *Guide to Jazz Improvisation,* published in 1968, differs greatly from the Aebersold chord-and-scale relationship method. LaPorta does not think students must master scales and chords in every key before undertaking jazz improvisation. He believes sounds should be addressed before theory and thus advocates the call-and-response technique for teaching improvisation. In his introduction, the first statement of purpose is "to improve the student's ability to effectively express a melodic idea." The terms "facility" and "technique" are used only in the fifth statement of purpose. The material on phrasing, ear training, and articulation is not obscured in a mass of scale and chord theory. LaPorta starts with jazz articulation. The lessons consist of learning two-measure rhythmic patterns and two-measure melodic patterns, which are then used in a short composition. Pentatonic scales are introduced in the first chapter and used throughout. Later, La Porta introduces blue notes. The student gradually learns to build extended melodic phrases by alternating longer sections of improvised material with the supplied written lines. The emphasis is on the melodic framework and on making short ideas sound "right."

A New Approach to Jazz Improvisation, by Steve and Ray Brown, relates the major scale with each of three chords: I, ii7, and V7. This simplifies learning because it helps the student make a connection between note choice and the chords in a ii7–V7–I Major 7th progression. Most of the play-along tracks are in a Latin style, dictating the use of even eighth-notes. One of the features of this method is that all of the rhythm section parts are notated: the piano voicings and rhythms, bass lines, guitar voicings and rhythms, and drum beats. The notated voicings and rhythms provide models for beginning improvisers as well as music teachers. The booklet also serves as an excellent combo guide to Latin and swing rhythms. There is a section on ii7–V7 progressions in which each progression is repeated numerous times.

The Beginning Improvisor, written by Ramon Ricker, is the first in a five-record set. The rhythm section's effective playing makes it very easy for a beginning improviser to find the pulse. Ricker makes the point that the student must use this method as a supplement to other jazz improvisational materials, practice, and listening. Ricker presents all of the major, Dorian, and Mixolydian scales and arpeggios in all keys and places emphasis on the chord and scale relationships. He addresses rhythm only briefly and does not address melodic development of the solo. Included are some rudimentary playing patterns to be used by the beginner for the ii7–V7 progressions. One of this volume's best features is the tenor saxophone melodies. The styles vary from a straight eighth-note to swing and are played at various tempos. Many of the melodies are modal, making them sound more contemporary. The level of difficulty progresses quickly from rather static harmonies to rhythm chord changes. This might prove difficult for a beginning improviser. There are other volumes in the collection that consists solely of jazz "standards."

Willie Thomas's *Jazz Anyone?* series has long been a mainstay for teaching blues-based improvisation to beginners on all instruments. *Fundamental Fun* is a blues-based method used with beginning concert band, string orchestra, or choir. Jazz rhythm is addressed at length, as is jazz phrasing. A group or individual may be taken step by step through this method. It is most important for a teacher with some improvisation skills to direct the students' work with this method. Little is mentioned about music theory.

Jazz Anyone? is concerned with two fundamentals of jazz: style and improvisation. The tapes provided give excellent examples of blues-based riffs for students to imitate. The examples become longer and more sophisticated, forcing students to imitate larger musical examples. There are also transcription exercises included providing students with more than enough material for practice. Imitation (call and response) is the primary focus of this method, not the chord-and-scale approach of the Aebersold series. As with *Fundamental Fun,* students need adequate musical supervision. Using Willie Thomas's methods for teaching jazz improvisation along with jazz theory probably would yield the best results.

The Art of Improvisation, by Rich Matteson and Jack Peterson, in two volumes, features the recorded rhythm section on one channel and recorded solos on the other. The listener has the option of using the recorded solos as models. The tracks progress by the addition of more frequent chord changes. Simple melodies are also provided. No written patterns or examples are given other than the notation of the scales used. The only examples provided are in the recorded solos on the right channel. The concept is good; however, some of the solos involve note choices and patterns not easily imitated by the beginner. The method's most notable feature is that it affords the beginner ample time to experiment in a few tonal centers. The swing-style melodies are simple, with little variation in tempo. This is a straightforward method that offers the beginner the opportunity to try new ideas.

The Music Company of North America has published three volumes of *Guest Soloist Series* play-alongs. These volumes are not methods per se, but collections of jazz compositions. Each volume contains compositions by a single composer, such as Stevie Wonder, Freddie Hubbard, and Chick Corea, and should be considered for the intermediate or advanced student.

Eight CD volumes available from Advance Music contain various jazz standards and some originals performed by an all-star jazz group. Each volume has two mixes: one with recorded solos, the other without. Volumes include:

Vol 1, *Modern Jazz Classics*

Vol 2, *Classic Jazz Standards*

Vol 3, *Blues—Standards and Originals*

Vol 4, *Quest—Standards and Originals*

Vol 5, *Modal Jazz—Standards and Originals*

Vol 6, *The Chick Corea Classics*

Vol 7, *I Hear a Rhapsody*

An unnumbered volume, *Blues and Rhythm Changes* by Fred Lipsius, is also available.

Also from Advance Music is *Creative Comping for Improvisation,* a three-volume series by Hal Crook. The only accompaniment is Crook playing a MIDI piano—no drums or bass. At first, the effect is startling without the drums and bass to keep time. While this forces the improviser to pay careful attention, it allows for more freedom once the progressions are mastered. Crook at times uses substitute chord changes, and the result is a challenge. The volumes contain only jazz standards.

Sher Music, publishers of *The New Real Book,* have issued a play-along series in three volumes. They include:

Vol 1, *Jazz Classics*

Vol 2, *Jazz Standards*

Vol 3, *Pop/Fusion*

David Berger's *Contemporary Jazz Studies* is a three-volume set based on chord progressions to popular jazz standards. Progressions of well-known compositions and written solos are to be performed over the recorded backgrounds. The written "etudes" start in a scale-wise manner, allowing the player to see and hear the chord and scale relationship. Each successive written chorus is more difficult, with broken arpeggios, complex rhythms, and then moving outside of the given chords. There is a wealth of written material for students to draw from in this volume to imitate and develop their vocabulary.

Teachers and students can choose from a wide variety of materials. The Aebersold method provides the widest variety of play-along materials ranging in difficulty from very easy to advanced. All of the methods above have advantages, but it is up to the individual to choose what works best.

Bibliography of Jazz Play-Along Materials

Advance Music Play-Alongs
Maierackerstr. 18
7407 Rottenburg, N. Germany
(also avail. Jamey Aebersold)

Alfred MasterTracks, Vol. I-IV
Blues, Fusion, Jazz, and Latin
Steve Houghton & Tom Warrington
Alfred Publishing Co., Inc.
P. O. Box 10003
Van Nuys, CA 91410-0003

The Art of Improvisation
Rich Matteson & Jack Peterson
Available through MMO

Beginning Improvisation Vol. I-III
Warner Brothers
15800 NW 48th Street
Miami, FL 33014

Club Date Sessions
Vol. I, Duke Ellington Collection
Warner Brothers
15800 NW 48th Street
Miami, FL 33014

Contemporary Jazz Studies
David Berger
Colin Publishers
15 W. 53rd Street
New York, NY 10019

Guest Soloist Series
The Music Company of North America
8211 Forest Hills Drive
Elkins Park, PA 19117

Guide to Improvisation
John LaPorta
Berklee Press
1140 Boylston Street
Boston, MA 02215

An Introduction to Jazz Improvisation
Steve and Ray Brown
Brown Cats Music
110 Eastwood Avenue
Ithaca, NY 14850

Jazz Anyone?
Willie Thomas
2517 St. Paul Street
Bellingham, WA 98226

Music Minus One
Theodore Front Musical Literature
50 Executive Boulevard
Elmsford, NY 10523

A New Approach to Improvisation
Jamey Aebersold
P. O. Box 1244C
New Albany, IN 47151-1244

New Real Book Play-Alongs
Sher Music Company
P. O. Box 445
Petaluma, CA 94953
(also avail. Jamey Aebersold)

A Selected List of Jazz Videos

Title	Type/ERA	Publisher	Artist	Instrument	Time (min.)
Anyone Can Improvise	Instructional	Aebersold	Jamey Aebersold	Instructional	120
Art Blakey: The Jazz Messenger	Documentary	Rhapsody Films	Art Blakey	Drums	60
Artistry in Rhythm	Third Stream	Aero Space	Stan Kenton	Big Band	60
Bill Evans	Mainstream	Rhapsody Films	Bill Evans	Piano	30
Buddy Rich Memorial Concert #1, 2, 3, 4	Post-Bop/ Mainstream	DCI Music Video	Buddy Rich/ various artists	Drums	60
Carmen McRae Live	Mainstream	Public Media Home Vision	Carmen McRae	Vocal	82
Celebrating Bird	Bebop	Kulture Int'l	Charlie Parker	Alto Sax	60
Como Su Ritmo No Hay Dos (His Rhythm is Like No Other)	Afro-Cuban	Crescent Moon/ Epic	Israel "Cachao" Lopez	Latin Jazz Ensemble/Bass	112
The Coltrane Legacy	Documentary	VAI Films	John Coltrane	Tenor/ Soprano Sax	60
A Different Drummer	Biography	Rhapsody Films	Elvin Jones	Drums	30
Electric Piano Workshop #1 & 2	Fusion	DCI Music Video	Chick Corea	Keyboard	60
The Evolution of Jazz Piano (2 Volumes)	Historical	Advanced Music	Bill Dobbins	Piano	60
The History of Jazz	Documentary	Insight Media	Billy Taylor	History	50
Freddie Hubbard at the Vanguard	Post-Bop	VAI Films	Freddie Hubbard	Trumpet	60
A Great Day in Harlem	Documentary	View	Various	Misc.	60
Hurricane	Mainstream/ Fusion	View Video	Herbie Hancock	Piano	60
Irakere: Live Performance	Afro-Cuban	Bembe, Descarga #TL-14363V	Irakere Small Band	Latin Jazz	55
Jaco Pastorius—Bass	Instructional	DCI Music Video	Jaco Pastorius	Instructional Bass	60
Jazz in Exile	Post-Bop/ Mainstream	Rhapsody Films	Various Artists	Misc.	60
Jazz Is My Language	Mainstream/ Modern	Rhapsody Films	Toshiko Akiyoshi	Big Band	60

Title	Type/ERA	Publisher	Artist	Instrument	Time (min.)
Jazz Lines	Instructional	DCI Music Video	Joe Pass	Guitar	60
Jazz Scene USA	Bebop	Shanachie Entertainment	Frank Rosolino Quartet/ Stan Kenton Orchestra Ensemble	Trombone/Jazz	60
Jobim: An All-Star Tribute	Brazilian	View Video 1349, Descarga #TL-14186V	Rubalcaba, Hancock Carter, Hendricks	Misc	60
John Abercrombie at the Vanguard	Post-Bop/ Mainstream	VAI Films	John Abercrombie	Guitar	60
Lady Day: The Many Faces of Billie Holiday	Documentary	Kultur Video & Intern'l Films	Billie Holiday	Vocal	60
The Ladies Sing the Blues	Documentary	View	Various Artists	Vocalists	60
Live in London	Bebop/ Afro-Cuban	Kultur 13350, Descarga #TL-14641V	Dizzy Gillespie	Jazz Ensemble/ Trumpet	91
Mal Waldron at the Vanguard	Avant-Garde	VAI Films	Mal Waldron	Piano	60
The Mambo King 100th LP	Afro-Cuban	Sony 89312 VID, Descarga # TL-9246V	Tito Puente	Latin Jazz Ensemble	68
Marsalis on Music, Vols. 1–4	Instructional	Sony Video	Marsalis Jazz Ensemble, Tanglewood Orchestra	Misc.	60
Mel Lewis and His Big Band	Big Band	View Inc.	Mel Lewis	Drums	38
Memories of Duke	Documentary	A*Vision Entertainment	Duke Ellington	Misc.	85
Michael Petrucciani at the Vanguard	Post-Bop/ Mainstream	VAI Films	Michael Petrucciani	Piano	60
Miles Davis in Paris	Modern	Warner Reprise	Miles Davis	Trumpet	60
The Music Tells You	Mainstream	SMV Enterprises	Branford Marsalis	Tenor Sax	60
New Bass Concepts	Instructional	BMG Video	Abraham Laboriel	Bass	60
New Stars on Blue Note	Mainstream	Blue Note Video	Various Artists	Misc.	60
A Night at Kimball's East	Afro-Cuban	Picante/Concord 44472, Descarga #TL-10708V	Poncho Sanchez Small Band	Latin Jazz	60

Title	Type/ERA	Publisher	Artist	Instrument	Time (min.)
Paris Reunion Band	Bebop	Proscenium Entertainment	Various Artists	Misc.	60
Phil Woods in Concert	Post-Bop	View Inc.	Phil Woods	Alto Sax	60
Piano Legends	Documentary	Video Artists	Various Artists	Piano	60
Reed Royalty	Documentary	Video Artists	Various Artists	Saxophone	60
Satchmo—The Life of Louis Armstrong	Biography	WNET New York CBS Movie Video VGB 2087-88	Louis Armstrong	Trumpet	87
Sarah Vaughan: The Divine One	Documentary	BMG Video	Sarah Vaughan	Vocal	60
Shelly Manne Quartet	Modern	Rhapsody Films	Shelly Manne	Jazz Quartet	30
Sonny Rollins Live	Progressive	Rhapsody Films	Sonny Rollins	Tenor Sax	30
The Sound of Jazz	Bebop/Swing	The Jazz Store	Monk, Young, Hawkins, Basie, etc.	Misc.	58
Stephane Grappelli in New Orleans	Mainstream	Leisure Enterprises, Ltd.	Stephane Grappelli	Violin	60
Straight No Chaser	Historical	Warner Bros.	Thelonious Monk	Piano	90
Street Beats (New Orleans Drumming)	Instructional	CCP Media/ Belwin	Johnny Vidacovich	Drums	65
Tal Farlow	Modern	Rhapsody Films	Tal Farlow	Guitar	60
Tenor Titans	Historical	Video Artists	Various Artists	Saxophone	60
Time Is Everything I	Instructional	VAI Films	Peter Erskine	Drums	60
Trumpet Kings	Documentary	VAI Films	Various Artists/ Wynton Marsalis	Misc./Trumpet	60
Wild Women Don't Have the Blues	Documentary	California	Various Newsreel	Misc.	58
Woody Herman Remembered	Big Band	Leisure Video	Woody Herman	Big Band	60
The World According to John Coltrane	Documentary	BMG Video	John Coltrane	Tenor Sax	60

Video Companies

Aebersold Music
P.O. Box 1244C
New Albany, IN 47151-1244

BMG Video
1540 Broadway
New York, NY 10036

California Newsreel
149 9th Street, #420
San Francisco, CA 94103

Caris Music Services
RD 7 Box 7621G
Stroudsburg, PA 18360

CPP Belwin
15800 NW 48th Avenue
Miami, FL 33014

DCI Music Video
541 Avenue of Americas
New York, NY 10011

Descarga
328 Flatbush Avenue, Suite 180
Brooklyn, NY 11238

Facets Video
1517 West Fullerton Avenue
Chicago, IL 60614

Frederic Weiner, Inc.
1325 2nd Avenue
New Hyde Park, NY 11040

Homespun Video
Box 694JT
Woodstock, NY 12498

Jazz Home Video Entertainment
P.O. Box 5207, Dept NJO
East Orange, NJ 07017

The Jazz Store
P.O. Box 917
Upper Montclair, NJ 07043

K–Twin Productions
1069 10th Avenue SE
Minneapolis, MN 55414

Kultur Video
121 Highway 36
W. Long Branch, NJ 07764

Leisure Enterprises, Ltd.
P.O. Box 56757, Dept. JT
New Orleans, LA 70156-6757

Media for the Arts
P.O. Box 1011
Newport, RI 02840

Mix Bookshelf
6400 Hollis Street, Suite #12
Emeryville, CA 94608

Public Media Home Vision
5547 N. Ravenswood Avenue
Chicago, IL 60640-1199

Rhapsody Films, Inc.
P.O. Box 179
New York, NY 10014

Shanachie Entertainment
P.O. Box 208
Newton, NJ 07860

Sony Video Software
1700 Broadway
New York, NY 10019

VAI Video
P.O. Box 153, Ansonia Station
New York, NY 10023

View Video
34 East 23rd Street
New York, NY 10010

Vintage Video
1631 East 79th Street, Suite 139
Minneapolis, MN 55425

Warner Vision Entertainment
75 Rockefeller Plaza
New York, NY 10019

A Selected List of Jazz Electronic Resources via Computer

There has been an exceptionally fast growth of resources available to the jazz educator with the advent of computer on-line services. The three primary avenues for this information exchange are bulletin boards, lists, and the World Wide Web. Many libraries are now also accessible via computer. To access these avenues, you generally need to have either a modem and on-line service (such as CompuServe, America On-line, etc.) or a direct line to the Internet (including its companion Bitnet and Usenet). Gopher and Telnet are other useful programs for accessing files and sites.

Bulletin Boards

"Bulletin boards" (also known as "newsgroups") are computer-generated sites for dialogue on a chosen topic by participants. An idea or question is posted, and other readers respond. This is an excellent location to pose a question for which you would like assistance from colleagues you have not yet met. It is common to view strings of responses as the original participants exchange thoughts and others join in. Each bulletin board focuses on a single topic; some of the ones most applicable to jazz and jazz education include the following:

alt.music a-cappella	(a cappella music, including jazz)
alt.music.midi	(MIDI use)
alt.radio.college	(radio programming)
comp.music	(all matters compositional and notational)
rec.music a-cappella	(a cappella music, including jazz)
rec.music.bluenote	(jazz)
rec.music.promotional	(music marketing)
rec.music.makers.songwriting	(song composition)

There are numerous boards related to world music, electronic music, and other jazz-related musics.

Lists

The network's "lists" are mailing lists to which you can subscribe for a regular flow of information and discussion. Some of the pertinent lists include:

CHORALIST@LISTS.COLORADO.EDU	(choral directors)
JAZZ@TEMPLEVM.BITNET	(jazz)
MILES@HEARN.BITNET	(Miles Davis)

There are lists devoted to each standard band instrument, MIDI instruments, voices, and more.

World Wide Web

Finally, the World Wide Web is a global network of computers. Many of its sites, or nodes, are cross-referenced at other related sites; so finding one or two nodes can lead you to a seemingly infinite series of linkages in the network. Such sites often contain historical information, discographies, sheet music volunteered by composers, lists of jazz media, files dedicated to individual artists or groups, and more.

Software to navigate the World Wide Web includes Mosaic and NetScape. Just enter the appropriate addresses, known as protocols. Some helpful sites include:

Entertainment Music: Jazz and Blues	http://akebono.stanfor.edu/yahoo /EntertainmentMusic/Jazz_and_Blues
IAJE Web site	http://jazzcentralstation.com/iaje
InterJazz	http://www.webcom.com/~ijazz/
Internet Underground Music Archive	http://www.iuma.com/
Jazz FanAttic	http://www2.magma_com.com/~rbour /jazz.htm
Jazz Links of the World	http://www.pk.edu/pl/~pmj/jazzlinks/
Jazz Online	http://www.jazzonln.com/JAZZ/
Jazz Resources	http://osiris.colorado.edu/~brumbaug /BCB/RES/jazz.html
Jazz Web	http://www.nwu.edu/WNUR/jazz/artists
MIDI Home Page	http://www.eeb.ele.tue.nl/midi/index.html
Music Resources on the Internet	http://www.music.indiana.edu /misc/music_resources.html
Oz-jazz Worldwide	http://magna.com/au/~georgeh/
WNUR-FM Jazz Information Server	http://www.nwu.edu/jazz/
World Wide Web Virtual Library: Music	http://www.oulu.fi./music.html
Yahoo! - Entertainment: Music:Genres: Jazz	http://www.yahoo.com/Entertainment /Music/Genres/Jazz/

Because this technology and its applications are fast developing, the information above may need to be updated. A host of books and articles are available on the subject. Some are shown here:

"Magical Musical Tours," *Electronic Musician,* Vol. 10, no. 10, October 1994, pp. 46–62.

"Multiculturalism, Music, and Information Highways," *Music Educators Journal,* Vol. 81, no. 3, November 1994, pp. 41–46.

For information on International Association of Jazz Educators (IAJE) and its programs, contact:

International Association of Jazz Educators
2803 Claflin Road
Manhattan, Kansas 66502
913-776-8744
fax: 913-776-6190
http://jazzcentralstation.com/iaje

For information on Music Educators National Conference (MENC) and its programs, contact:

Music Educators National Conference
1806 Robert Fulton Drive
Reston, VA 20191-4348
703-860-4000
fax: 703-860-1531
http://www.menc.org